A GUIDE TO BRITISH CAVALRY UNIFORMS AND BADGES IN OLD PRINTS, PICTURES AND POSTCARDS,

1660 TO 1914

A GUIDE TO BRITISH CAVALRY UNIFORMS AND BADGES IN OLD PRINTS, PICTURES AND POSTCARDS,

1660 to 1914

by Ray Westlake

The Naval & Military Press

For James Westlake

© Ray Westlake 2021

Published by

The Naval & Military Press Ltd
Unit 5 Riverside
Bellbrook Industrial Estate
Uckfield, East Sussex
TN22 1QQ England

Tel: +44 (0) 1825 749494

www.naval-military-press.com

CONTENTS

Acknowledgments viii

Introduction ix

The Cavalry Regiments 1

Bibliography 77

ACKNOWLEDGMENTS

This book would not have been possible without the help of the Anne SK Brown Military Collection held at Brown University, Providence, Rhode Island, USA. You will see their name at the end of each of the images that they have generously allowed me to use in this work. Also essential to this project was my guide in all things, my wife Claire, an expert deleter of commas and semi-colons.

INTRODUCTION

There is much to be learnt from pictures. It was film producer and pioneer of the American animation industry Walt Disney who said, 'Of all of our inventions for mass communication, pictures still speak the most universally understood language.' And, of course, we must not forget the wider use of, 'A picture is worth a thousand words.' Certainly, if we set out to make a study of uniform, we can learn much from looking at pictures. But, as that superb reference work published by the Army Museums Ogilby Trust in 1972, *Index To British Military Costume Prints 1500-1914*, points out, '…it must not be supposed that a contemporary artist, however celebrated, does not make mistakes in drawing what he thought he had seen.' To this we could add, 'or what he thought might look good'—artistic licence, in fact. Here, as an example, I bring to mind a comment made by none less that Richard Caton Woodville who after the end of the Great War was given a commission by the London Scottish to paint a picture recalling that regiment's brave stand at Messines Ridge at the end of October 1914. Up in the Mess went the finished article. Those who were there pointed out recognisable faces and features of the battle and in general were pleased at what they saw. But up stepped one veteran who with finger pointing exclaimed, 'They're wearing sporrans. We never had them on the Ridge, they were left behind at our billets.' This point was raised with the artist who remarked without hesitation, 'Yes, I'm quite aware of this. I included them as I thought the men looked quite empty without them.'

At this point the serious student of military dress may well abandon the idea of including prints and pictures in his study of the subject, and instead content him or herself with official publications such as Dress or Clothing Regulations. But, before the critic condemns an artist for depicting a uniform that was never approved under the regulations (*Index to British Military Costume Prints* again), let him remember that the 'British officer has long been noted for his independence from Dress Regulations.'

With all that said, let us now set about enjoying what talented people have placed on paper and canvas for centuries. How wonderful it must have been to have called into Rudolph Ackermann's shop at 96 Strand, London in the 1790s to purchase something from his vast stock of military or sporting prints. And equally, in more recent times, was the Parker Gallery at 2 Albemarle Street, Piccadilly where you could treat yourself to something of the old regiment to go up above the living room fireplace. Here then, for each cavalry regiment is a small selection of informative, or just a delight to look at, images.

1st and 2nd Life Guards

Titles
Regimental lineage regarding the Life Guards is somewhat complex, but authority of the subject JBM Frederick in his *Lineage Book of British Land Fores 1660-1987* provides the following account: the 1st or His Majesty's Own Troop of Guards raised 1658 in Holland amongst exiled followers of Charles II. We then have the 3rd, or the Duke of Albermarle's Troop of Guards raised 1659 in the Spanish Service as Monk's Life Guards and designated 1660 as the Lord General's Troop of Guards, then re-designated in 1670 as the 2nd (The Queen's) Troop. Turning now to another reliable authority, Arthur Swinson and *A Register of the Regiments and Corps of the British Army,* we read that by an order of 26 January 1661 Charles II established his Household Cavalry comprising: His Majesty's Own Troop, a Duke of York's Troop and a third known as the Duke of Albermarle's. By 1788 there were only two troops and it was these that in that year were designated as two separate regiments—the 1st and 2nd Life Guards.

Battle Honours
'Dettingen', 'Peninsular', 'Waterloo', 'Tel-el-Kebir', 'Egypt 1882', 'Relief of Kimberley', 'Paardeberg', 'South Africa 1899-1900'

Recommended Further Reading
Historical Record of the Life Guards; Containing an Account of the Formation of the corps in the Year 1660, and its Subsequent Services to 1835, prepared for publication under the direction of the Adjutant General, London 1835. Contains six colour plates of uniform. For a first class uniform reference, see *The Dress of the First Regiment of Life Guards in Three Centuries* by UHR Broughton, published in London by Halton & Truscott-Smith, Ltd in 1925 with some forty coloured plates.

Images

1 – 1st Troop of Horse Guards, 1751 Historian WY Carman points out that early uniform detail is scant, but refers to the engravings by Wenceslas Hollar which shows the King's Troop wearing buff coats with white armour, red scarfs and red-and-white feather plumes at the king's coronation. The Duke of York's Troop had black armour and black-and-white feathers in their hats. By 1669, records Mr Carman, both troops had white feathers and red jackets faced with blue. The King's had gold lace, but none for the Duke's. The 3rd, Albermarle's Troop was dressed similar to the Duke's, but with crimson ribbons instead of feathers.

Illustrated is an original watercolour painting by Richard Simkin which shows a private of the 1st

AN OFFICER of the 2.d REGIMENT of LIFE GUARDS. in full Dress.

King's Troop. The black soft felt hat is edged with gold lace, the coat having blue lapels, also with gold lace edging, blue cuffs and turnbacks. The long waistcoat and gauntlet gloves are buff. The royal cypher with crown above appears on the holster-caps and shabraque which are both scarlet with two lines of gold lace. *(Image courtesy of the Anne SK Brown Military Collection, Brown University Library)*

2 – An Officer of the 2nd Regiment of Life Guards in Full Dress Drawn and etched by Charles Hamilton Smith and included, after aquatinting by IC Stadler, in the *Costumes of the Army of the British Empire* series published in London between March 1812 and June 1815 by Colnaghi & Co of Cockspur Street and printed by W Bulmer & Co of Cleveland Row. This plate appeared in July 1812, that year being that in which two squadrons from each of the 1st and 2nd Life Guards were sent to Portugal. Troops had arrived at Lisbon on 23 November and there formed into a brigade, together with the Royal Horse Guards, under the overall command of Major-General Francis Slater Rebow of the Life Guards. The battle of Vittoria followed on 21 June and the autumn and winter of 1813 were spent in quarters at Logroño. Both regiments had returned to London by 8 February 1816 with the battle honours 'Peninsula' and 'Waterloo'.

Charles Hamilton Smith shows the officer leading a charge over high ground. His troops follow, one carrying a standard which catches the breeze as the advance gathers speed. In the near distance, a trumpeter sounding the 'Charge' can be seen mounted on a grey. The lapels of the jacket are covered in gold lace which conceals the regiment's dark blue facing colour. The tails too show much gold and white turnbacks. Note how the holster-caps and shabraque both have a blue line between gold lace, this a distinction of the 2nd Life Guards. The 1st had scarlet. Also seen in the image is a crimson sash and black sheepskin saddle cover.

3 – 1st Life Guards Marching in Horse Guards Parade, c1837 Fur caps were introduced, notes uniform authority WY Carman, for parades after 1820. Helmets were, however, retained. Here in this original watercolour painting by Richard Simkin we see a parade at Horse Guards in London, the white pouch-belts with their red flack-cords identifying the troops as being from the 1st Life Guards. The 2nd would have blue. Unseen in the image being worn by the officer in the centre is his elaborate crimson and gold waist-sash, but visible are its two heavy tassels.

4 – 1st and 2nd Life Guards c 1850 In this original watercolour by W Sharpe, which also included an officer of the Royal Horse Guards, we see representations of both 1st and 2nd Life Guards, the German silver helmets, steel cuirasses and uniforms offering a scene not too far removed from that which can be seen at Horse Guards Parade during the daily guard changing ceremony. We have seen how the two regiments can be identified by the central stripes running through the pouch-belts—red for 1st Life Guards, blue for the 2nd.

There are other distinctions, however, and for descriptions of these we now turn to contemporary Dress Regulations. For the shoulder straps we have: '1st Regiment, brass scale, lined with scarlet cloth, 2nd Regiment, gold embroidery on scarlet cloth, solid gilt crescent, and blue centre, padded with blue cloth.' There are none in the image, but the cloaks varied too, both scarlet, Dress Regulations give: 'Blue collar and cape, for 1st Regiment; blue collar and scarlet cape, for 2nd Regiment.' But more noticeable possibly are the officers' shabraques: pointed ends for the 1st Life Guards, rounded for the 2nd. Just hinted at in W Sharpe's painting is the red silk stripe worked into the outer edge of the 1st Regiment's gold lace. Clearer in the image is the scarlet cloth ground distinction to the shabraque lace of the 2nd regiment which can be seen forming a half-inch edging.

There are differences in the embroidery, too. 1st Life Guards: 'On the hind-corners, a garter star proper, above which is a double cypher, L.G., surmounted by a scroll, bearing the words, "Peninsula, Waterloo," and a gold crown above all. On the front corners, the double cypher, L.G., surmounted by a small figure "1" and a gold crown above all.' And for the 2nd Regiment: 'On the hind corners, a garter tar proper, with the figure "2" beneath it, and on the sides a gold laurel branch, bearing the words, "Peninsula," 'Waterloo," the Queen's crest above all. On the front corners the same, except the figure "2." *(Image courtesy of the Anne SK Brown Military Collection, Brown University Library)*

Royal Horse Guards (The Blues)

Titles
1661 – Royal Regiment of Horse. Also known as the Oxford Blues
1687 – Royal Regiment of Horse Guards
1750 – Royal Horse Guards (Blue)
1819 – Royal Regiment of Horse Guards (The Blues)
1877 – Royal Horse Guards (The Blues)

Battle Honours
'Dettingen', 'Warburg', 'Beaumont', 'Willems', 'Peninsula', 'Waterloo', 'Tel-el-Kebir', 'Egypt 1882', 'Relief of Kimberley', 'Paardeberg', 'South Africa 1899-1900'

Recommended Further Reading
An Historical Record of the Royal Regiment of Horse Guards or Oxford Blues, its Services, and the Transactions in which it has been engaged, from its first Establishment to the Present Time, by Edmund Packe and published in London by William Clowes in 1834. Contains six colour plates of uniform. Another edition was published as part of the Cannon's Historical Records' series in 1847, the publisher this time being Parker, Furnivall & Parker of London. Contains seven colour plates of uniform.

Images

1 – The Blues Published on 1 February 1823 by SW Fores of 41 Piccadilly, London, this 24.5 x 36.5 cm aquatint is one of a set of four after William Heath (1795-1840) held at the Anne SK Brown Military Collection, Brown University Library, Providence, Rhode Island, USA. The etching was done by Joshua Gleadah. With a mountainous backdrop, a long line of troops wearing light blue jackets and white trousers can be seen in the near distance. A soldier with his back to us looks out across a wide-open space to the men as three of his brother officers stand in conversation.

In 1820, records uniform historian WY Carman, George IV had granted the Royal Horse Guards the same honours and privileges as those enjoyed by the two regiments of Life Guards, the post-Waterloo years seeing '…an opportunity to introduce new uniforms worthy of the victorious troops.' So now the uniforms of the Royal Horse Guards were to closely assimilate those of the 1st and 2nd Life Guards, the main difference being that the colours were reversed—blue with scarlet facings as opposed to the scarlet and blue of the Life Guards. In the central figure, which is shown in full mounted dress, we see the 'Roman' helmet introduced in 1817 with its tall black bearskin crest. A coatee with long tails and a high scarlet collar decorated with gold lace is being worn with large gold epaulettes. The red scalloped lining of the cuirass is clearly visible in the painting as it protrudes at the neck, armholes and waist. A scarlet flask-cord runs centrally through a white pouch-belt which is worn across the left shoulder. Plaited gold aiguillettes, a gold and scarlet sash ending with long tassels, white leather breeches and gauntlet gloves, and tall black boots rising to just above the knee are also being worn.

The officer on the right, who wears undress uniform, has a broad-crowned black forage cap with gold lace band. The single-breasted blue frock coat has gold shoulder cords and is worn belted at the waist. The overalls are bright blue with a wide red stripe. The all-blue uniform of the officer standing on the left is highly decorated with gold lace, his headdress being the cocked hat which, when removed, could be carried flat under the arm. *(Image courtesy of the Anne SK Brown Military Collection, Brown University Library)*

2 – Royal Regiment of Horse Guards, 1834 In this original watercolour by George Edward Madeley (1798-1858) we see the bearskin cap worn from 1833 to 1842. There is a long feather positioned on the left side of the headdress which runs across the top and just down the right. To make a distinction from the Life Guards, the feather is red instead of white.

For a detailed description of the uniform we now turn to *Regulations for the Dress of the General Staff and Regimental Officers of The Army* published in 1834 by William Clowes & Sons: *Coat* – blue, single-breasted; one row of eight buttons in front placed at equal distances; scarlet cloth Prussian collar, embroidered in front; scarlet cloth pointed cuff, open at the side, with two embroidered loops; an edging of scarlet cloth down the front of the coat and round the waist, the skirt with straight flap on the hip, edged with scarlet cloth, and two buttons, also two in centre of back; scarlet turnbacks, and embroidered skirt ornaments.' The epaulettes are gold bullion three inches deep and the aiguillette worn on the right shoulder is of twisted gold cord with gilt engraved tags. Regarding the fur cap, this is described as: 'black bear-skin, fourteen inches deep in front, with gold two inch and a half bullion tassels on the right side; a gilt grenade in the front, having the King's arms raised upon the centre; gilt leaf scales, attached to the cap by large lion-head roses, and clasped at the ends by a small rose of the same pattern.' The red swan's feather is twenty-four inches in length.

The horse furniture is scarlet with a border of two rows of gold lace divided by a strip of light blue cloth. Unclear in the image is the embroidery of a crown and star together with the battle honours 'Waterloo' and 'Peninsular'. *(Image courtesy of the Anne SK Brown Military Collection, Brown University Library)*

3 – Royal Horse Guards, Officers c1875 Signed by Richard Simkin and dated 1875, this original watercolour shows two officers, one in state dress, the other wearing a stable jacket. Looking much like he would today, the mounted officer's German steel helmet has a scarlet horsehair plume and gilt and silver fittings, the badge being the Garter star. The cuirass is of polished steel, ornamented with brass studs. The pouch-belt is gold lace lined with scarlet Morocco leather showing a stripe in the centre. The shabraque is of scarlet cloth with its fore corners rounded and hind corners pointed. The two stripes of gold lace show quarter-inch blue cloth between. Here again is the regiment's Garter star badge. The dress of the dismounted officer includes a blue cloth stable-jacket with scarlet collar and cuffs. The gold lace is one inch wide. *(Image courtesy of the Anne SK Brown Military Collection, Brown University Library)*

1st (King's) Dragoon Guards

Titles
1685 – The Queen's (or 2nd) Regiment of Horse
1714 – The King's Own Regiment of Horse
1746 – The 1st King's Dragoon Guards

Battle Honours
'Blenheim', 'Ramillies', 'Oudenarde', 'Malplaquet', 'Dettingen', 'Warburg', 'Beaumont', 'Waterloo', 'Sevastopol', 'Taku Forts', 'Pekin 1860', 'South Africa 1879', 'South Africa 1901-02'

RECOMMENDED FURTHER READING

Historical Record of the First, or King's Regiment of Dragoon Guards by Richard Cannon and published by William Clowes & Sons in 1837. Includes four colour plates of uniform. By the Rev Percy Summer, a comprehensive article on the regiment's uniforms and equipment appeared in Volume 13 of the *Journal of the Society for Army Historical Research* published in 1934.

IMAGES

1 – The Queen's Regiment of Horse, 1688 The Queen's Regiment of Horse was raised of nine troops in 1685 by a warrant dated 13 June, its first colonel being Sir John Lanier whose commission was dated 6 June. For uniform detail at the time we turn to Richard Cannon who gives the coats as red with yellow facings. He also notes that the men wore jacked leather boots, buff gauntlets and shoulder belts, cuirasses and iron head-pieces called pots. Each troop at the time had richly embroidered yellow satin standards, the cost of these being on record as £40 6s 8d. The trumpeters too (two per troop) were richly clothed at a cost of £36 12s 2d.

Illustrated is a watercolour by Richard Simkin dated 1688 which shows a mounted officer in red and yellow. Sword drawn, he wears a wide black hat edged with silver lace and sporting a large white feather. A steel cuirass is worn (discarded by the regiment in 1689), and a crimson sash is tied around the waist. The coat is edged with silver, as are the pockets and cuffs. During the summer of 1688, the regiment was quartered on Hounslow Heath in Middlesex, a move being made towards the end of the year to Colnbrook, Chertsey and Byfleet. At Oxford, on 15 December, Princess Anne (later Queen Anne) made a public entry into the city, the cavalcade which attended including the Queen's Regiment of Horse.

The regiment was also known as the 2nd Regiment of Horse, becoming the King's Own Regiment of Horse in 1714 and the 1st (King's) Dragoon Guards in 1746. *(Image courtesy of the Anne SK Brown Military Collection, Brown University Library)*

2 – A Private of the 1st or King's Dragoon Guards With this illustration we move forward to 1812 and the publication in March that year of a Charles Hamilton Smith drawing featuring a private of the 1st or King's Dragoons Guards. The artist also etched the work, passing it on for aquatinting to IC Stadler. The regimental blue facing colour can be seen on the collar, gold laced shoulder straps, coat front, girdle and turnbacks. The lace is yellow, that running up the front of the coat terminating on each side with red patches on the collar.

Helmets of black felt, with brass peaks and brass bars at the side to provide strength, have replace the wide hats edged with silver as seen in image 1. Brass too is used for the ornamental fitting supporting the worsted crest. The cypher GR with crown above can be seen on the helmet plate. This pattern of headwear had been introduced via a warrant dated 12 March 1812, its approval following on 20 March. Just distinguishable on the blue horse furniture, which has two lines of gold lace around the edges, is a red and gold embroidered crown above an intertwined and reversed GR cypher above the letters KD over G. The same lettering also appears on the scarlet tubular valise carried at the rear of the saddle. Note the metal spring clip attached to the wide white leather shoulder belt. For safety, the carbine seen here held in position via a leather cup device called a 'boot' at the rider's right side, and with its lock mechanism covered, could be fixed to this so as to prevent loss during action.

3 – Kettledrummer and Drum Horse The regiment returned from India, where it had been stationed since 1885, in 1891 and it was about this time that the blue drum banners bearing the Royal Arms seen in the illustration were taken into use. Laurel sprays carrying five battle honours are placed on either side, 'Waterloo' appearing separately below and above the title King's Dragoon Guards. The kettledrummer wears gold aiguillettes and a white helmet plume in lieu of the regimental red. The illustration is after Frederick Stansell and from WJ Gordon's book, *Bands of the British Army*.

'After the regiment returned to this country from the South African War in 1903', records RG Harris in his splendid series of articles on mounted bands, drum horses and banners published by the Military Historical Society, 'they were quartered at Hounslow and subsequently at Aldershot. It was here in August 1904, that their piebald drum-horse was

transferred to the 11th Hussars.' To take its place was the grey seen in Frederick Stansell's painting. Harris also notes that the kettle drummer was a private with a long service chevron and we can see him here wearing the regiment's double-headed eagle collar badge.

4 – What Power is it That Mounts my Love so High? About 1880, the London and New York publisher George Routledge & Sons produced a wonderful book of cartoons under the title of *Military Misreadings of Shakspere*. The exclusion of the first 'e' and second 'a' in the title are an alternative version of the Bard's name. Authorship, and indeed the artwork, is credited to a 'Major Seccombe'—Thomas Strong Seccombe (1840-1913), in fact, a British

Royal Artillery officer well known for several books of cartoons and caricatures. This volume takes Shakespearean quotes (from *All's Well that Ends Well:* Act 1, scene 1 in this case) and places them together with humorous artwork featuring military men in uniform. Is the King's Dragoon Guards officer's 'love' the concerned lady looking through the window across a jungle of potted plants…or his horse?

2ND DRAGOON GUARDS (QUEEN'S BAYS)

TITLES
1685 – Colonel the Earl of Peterborough's Regiment of Horse
1688 – 3rd Regiment of Horse
1715 – Princess of Wales's Own Royal Regiment of Horse
1727 – Queen's Own Royal Regiment of Horse
1746 – 2nd Queen's Dragoon Guards
1872 – 2nd Dragoon Guards (Queen's Bays)

BATTLE HONOURS
'Warburg', 'Willems', 'Lucknow', 'South Africa 1901-02'

RECOMMENDED FURTHER READING
Historical Record of the Second, or Queen's Regiment of Dragoon Guards (Queen's Bays). Part of the Cannon's 'Historical Records' series which covers the history of the regiment from formation in 1685 to 1837. Published in London by William Clowes & Sons, the book has four colour plates of uniform. Taking the history from 1685 up to 1929 is Frederic Whyte and A Hilliard Atteridge's *A History of the Queen's Bays (The 2nd Dragoon Guards)*, published by Jonathan Cape in London, 1930. There are eight colour plates of uniform.

IMAGES
1 – 2nd Dragoon Guards by Reginald Augustus Wymer The earliest figure (see bottom right) in this original watercolour by Reginald Augustus Wymer (1849-1935) seems to have been misdated by the artist as 1646. The regiment was not formed until 1685 and Richard Cannon tells us how that in June that year James, Duke of Monmouth, with a band of armed followers, had arrived in England intent on claiming the throne as his own. In support of the king, quickly a number of independent troops of cavalry formed: one by Sir Michael Wentworth at

Wakefield and Pontefract, another by Sir John Talbot around Hounslow in Middlesex, a third by John Lloyd in the Edgware area, and a fourth by Lord Aylesbury in London and its surrounding area. It was these four troops that were incorporated into a regiment of horse commanded by Henry, the second Earl of Peterborough.

Regarding uniform: 'The regiment being completed to its numbers' (Cannon again), 'was clothed, armed, and equipped as a Corps of Cuirassiers. The men were clothed in scarlet, lined with the same colour; they wore hats bound with silver lace and ornamented with ribands; and large boots which came up to the middle of the thigh.' Richard Cannon included with his record of the 2nd Dragoon Guards a colour plate showing a mounted

officer dressed much the same as Wymer's lower right figure, placing with it the caption 'Third Horse, 1687. Constituted Second Dragoon Guards, 1746.' Basing his painting on that of Cannon's, could it be that Wymer had misread 1746 for 1646?

Wymer's next figure (bottom left and dated 1742) has been based on official records and now shows the coat with wide buff lapels, the same colour also being used for the shoulder belt, gauntlet glove, shoulder straps and horse furniture, the latter having gold lace with a central scarlet stripe and a crowned Garter with royal cypher. Unseen in the image is the waistcoat which was also buff, as were the linings of the scarlet rolled cloak.

Moving now to the top left, we find a similar mounted figure to that below, this time dated 1760. Once again the colour buff is much in evidence, clearly seen now is the waistcoat, but now we have two shoulder-belts, one with a flask cord, and horse furniture this time decorated with a trophy of arms, flags, drums, lances etc.

Quite a different uniform is shown at top right. Dated 1828 we now have a coatee highly decorated with silver lace and cord, across the chest, on the collar, shoulders and forming chevron lines, each with two silver buttons, on the lower arms. The collar and cuffs are now of black velvet. Silver lace too for the blue-grey trousers. But in 1830 it was ordered that officers of the regular forces should wear gold lace, the silver now being a distinction of the Militia and Volunteers. Here we see it, on the collar, shoulder straps, belts, trousers and horse furniture of Wymer's central figure dated 1837.

2 – Officers' Full Dress Helmet The blackened helmet with its bearskin crest being worn by the officer at the centre of Wymer's painting above, was featured in a set of cigarette cards published in 1931 by John Player & Sons. Here we see it with its gilt fittings, just as shown by Wymer.

3 – 2nd Dragoon Guards, 1794 In this illustration artist Charles Lyall shows a member of the regiment wearing a scarlet coat closed to the waist, its long tails showing white turnbacks. The collar and wide lapels are blue with silver or white lace or braid. The black felt hat has silver or white tassels, a black cockade and tall white over red feather plume. *(Image courtesy of the Anne SK Brown Military Collection, Brown University Library)*

4 – 2nd Dragoon Guards, c1885 The officer featured in this original watercolour by Richard Simkin wears a scarlet tunic, its buff collar being decorated with ¾-inch gold lace. The shoulder straps

are of plaited flat gold cord lined with scarlet cloth. The helmet is gilt brass with a black horsehair plume, the helmet plate being a diamond cut silver star. On this, a gilt metal Garter and motto. Within this on a red enamel ground, the Royal Cypher in silver. A gold lace waist-belt is being worn which has Morocco leather lining and a buff velvet edging. The rectangular plate has in the centre the Royal Cypher and Crown encircled with oak leaves. *(Image courtesy of the Anne SK Brown Military Collection, Brown University Library)*

5 – Band of the 2nd Dragoon Guards (Queen's Bays) Headed by the regimental band, the 2nd Dragoon Guards (Queen's Bays) turn a sharp corner into a dusty lane. The column is led by the regiment's drum horse, the kettle drummer being shown as a corporal who wears white aiguillettes from the left shoulder. The drum banner is buff, following the facing colour of the Bays, and carried below the gold embroidered wreath the single battle honour, 'Lucknow'. The shabraque is blue with gold lace and carries, as the drum banner, the word 'Bays' in old English lettering. Note how the helmet plumes of the band are white in marked contrast to those of the regimental which are black. The print is from *Our Armies*, illustrated and described by Richard Simkin.

3rd (Prince of Wales's) Dragoon Guards

Titles
1685 – Colonel The Earl of Plymouth's Regiment of Horse
1687 – 4th Regiment of Horse

1746 – 3rd Regiment of Dragoon Guards
1765 – 3rd (Prince of Wales's) Dragoon Guards

Battle Honours
'Blenheim', 'Ramillies', 'Oudenarde', 'Malplaquet', 'Warburg', 'Beaumont', 'Willems', 'Talavera', 'Albuhera', 'Vittoria', 'Peninsula', 'Abyssinia', 'South Africa 1901-02'

Recommended Further Reading
Historical Record of the Third, or Prince of Wales's Regiment of Dragoon Guards. Part of the Richard Cannon 'Historical Records' series, published in London by William Clowes & Sons, 1838. Contains two colour plates of uniform.

Images
1 – 4th Regiment of Horse, 1687 With the 1685 rebellion of the Duke of Monmouth, several noblemen loyal to the king raised independent troops of cavalry for his service: Thomas Earl of Plymouth in

Worcestershire, Claudius Earl of Abercorn throughout Oxfordshire, Henry Lord Eyland at St Alban's, Henry Lord Grey in Bedfordshire, Lionel Walden in the area of Huntingdon and Ambrose Brown in the neighbourhood of Dorking. It was these six troops that, after the capture and execution of Monmouth, were formed into a regiment of horse ranked as 4th with the colonelcy going to the Earl of Plymouth.

Historian Richard Cannon recalled the uniform adopted: 'The men wore hats with broad brims, bound with silver lace, turned up on one side and ornamented with green ribands; scarlet coats lined with green shallon, and high boots made of jacked leather.' The writer also recorded how they had scarlet cloaks lined with green, and green horse furniture embroidered with white, and ornamented with the king's cypher and crown. Illustrated is one of the hand-coloured plates included with Cannon's *Records of the Third Dragoon Guards* and as can be seen, it fits quite accurately with the author's description which adds the remark that the cuirasses 'were pistol-proof....'

2 – 4th Regiment of Horse, 1742 In this original watercolour by Richard Simkin we see that the green facing colour had now changed to white. Both the coat and breeches are red, the waistcoat white. Exactly when white replaced the original green has not been recorded but the colour, notes uniform authority WY Carman, was in use by the time of an image that appeared in the Duke of Cumberland's *Clothing Book* of 1742. Buff leather belts and gauntlet gloves are also being worn in Simkin's painting, the carbine belt having a white flask cord running through its centre.

3 – 3rd Dragoon Guards, 1845 In this lithograph from the Anne SK Brown Military Collection, we see a mounted officer holding the helmet introduced around 1843, 'Gilt brass', records *Regulations for the Dress of General Staff and Regimental Officers of the Army* in 1846, 'with regimental ornaments and devices in front, and an ornamental crest (three inches and a half deep) in which is inserted a mane of black horsehair (two feet ten inches long) flowing loose behind and terminating in front in a thistle-shaped brush, confined by a gold embroidered boss, gilt brass scales.' The scarlet coat has nine buttons down the front (two hidden by the belt) and gold bullion epaulettes. Unseen on the latter is the regimental badge of the plumes and coronet of the Prince of Wales. The waist-belt is of gold lace, two inches and a half wide, the rectangular plate being the same width and bearing the device of a silver 'VR' cypher surmounted by a crown and encircled with oak leaves. The pouch-belt, worn over the left shoulder, is of the same material and width as that worn around the waist. The sabretache is the yellow of the now facing colour and is edged all round with gold. On the blue shabraque at the front, the Prince of Wales's plumes, coronet and motto.

The artist (unknown in this case) has also provided a back view of an officer which illustrates how well down the back came the black horsehair mane, and how the sabretache almost reached the ground when dismounted. *(Image courtesy of the Anne SK Brown Military Collection, Brown University Library)*

4 – 3rd (Prince of Wales's) Dragoon Guards, 1909 The Anne SK Brown Military Collection are fortunate in as much has they hold a number of original artworks produced for commercial postcard sets. Signed Ernest Ibbetson and dated 1909, we have a fine study of a mounted private of the regiment and a sergeant. In both, the regiment's yellow facing colour is much in evidence, the shoulder straps being embroidered with the title '3' over 'DG' in red. Clearly seen on the collars is the regiment's Prince of Wales's plumes, coronet and motto badge, which is also worn above the chevrons of non-commissioned-officers. The sergeant's cap has a yellow band and welt around the top. The regiment's helmet plume had changed to black and red by 1855. Both men wear medals awarded for service during the Second Boer War. The eventual postcard was published by the Aldershot firm of Gale & Polden. *(Image courtesy of the Anne SK Brown Military Collection, Brown University Library)*

5 – Kettledrummer, 3rd Dragoon Guards Mr RG Harris in his splendid series of articles, 'Mounted Bands, Their Drum-Horses and Banners', written for the Military Historical Society during the 1960s, refers to a note by F Stansell which tells how the 3rd Dragoon Guards had had their drum-banners and shabraque stolen by natives whilst serving in India. The regiment was stationed there from 1857 to 1867 and again from 1884 to 1892. After a tour of duty in South Africa, the regiment returned home in 1895 and photographs taken at Aldershot in 1896 show that the drum-horse was a piebald just like that shown by Stansell. The animal had been obtained from the 20th Hussars in October 1895. There was at the time, however, still no drum-banners.

It is thought that the new drum-banners (RG Harris again) shown in the illustration were obtained for the Diamond Jubilee celebrations in 1897. Of yellow velvet, the Prince of Wales' plumes, coronet and motto featured with the designation 'III DG' in the centre of a union wreath of roses, thistles and shamrocks. Below this was the battle honour 'Abyssinia' on a scroll. Other honours—'Blenheim', 'Ramillies', 'Oudenarde', 'Malplaquet', 'Talavera', 'Albuhera', 'Vittoria' and 'Peninsula'—were displayed four on either side of the wreath. The illustration is from *Bands of the British Army* by WJ Gordon, published by Frederick Warne & Co, Ltd around 1914 with illustrations after Frederick Stansell. It is indeed a magnificent book which shows the mounted kettledrummers of all thirty-one cavalry regiments in twelve chromoliths together with images of infantry bandsmen.

4th (Royal Irish) Dragoon Guards

Titles
1685 – Colonel the Earl of Arran's Regiment of Horse, also known as 6th Horse
1690 – 5th Horse
1746 – 1st Irish Horse, also known as Blue Horse
1788 – 4th Dragoon Guards, changing to 4th (Royal Irish) Dragoon Guards in the same year

Battle Honours
'Peninsula', 'Balaclava', 'Sevastopol', 'Tel-el-Kabir', 'Egypt 1882'

Recommended Further Reading
Historical Record of the Fourth, or Royal Irish Regiment of Dragoon Guards by Richard Cannon and published by Longman, Orme & Co, London, 1839. Contains two colour plates of uniform.

Images

1 – Colonel Langston's 5th Horse, 1693 It was James Earl of Arran, the eldest son of William Duke of Hamilton, who in 1685 had gathered the regiment's first troop together in the north of England. Others soon followed in the vicinity of London, Lichfield, Grantham, Durham and Morpeth and it would be these together that formed a regiment of horse ranked as 6th in the British line. Numerical titles had not yet been introduced into the British Army and it followed that the regiment became known as Arran's Cuirassiers, the Earl having received the colonelcy by commission dated 28 July 1685. Referring now to Richard Cannon's history we learn that the corps was 'composed of the sons of substantial yeomen and tradesmen, who provided their own horses,' the author going on to say how the regiment was held in high estimation throughout the country and how the men enjoyed a rate of pay (two shillings and six pence per day) which provided them with 'a respectable station in society.'

Richard Cannon provides details regarding the arms, dress and equipment of the Earl of Arran's Regiment, mentioning that it possessed, in common with the other regiments of cuirassiers, long swords, a pair of long pistols, and short carbines. Hats, decorated with ribands, were worn which had broad brims, bound with narrow lace and turned up on one side. The regiment was distinguished by white ribands, white linings to their red coats, white waistcoats and breeches and white horse furniture. The officers had white sashes.

Having been ordered to Ireland in 1698, the regiment now ranked as 5th Horse landed at Dublin on 31 March where it was placed on the Irish establishment. When the change in its distinguishing colour went from white to blue is not clear. Richard Cannon gives a date of around 1715 and certainly white was recorded during a review held at Hounslow Heath in 1686. There is, however, an original

watercolour by Charles James Lydall (1845-1920) dated 1693 and captioned 'Colonel Langston's Fifth Horse' in the Anne SK Brown Military Collection which shows a mounted figure with long scarlet coat, blue cuffs edged with wide gold lace and wearing a wide-brimmed hat with a double white feather plume. The officer wears a steel cuirass with gilt fittings, white breeches tucked into high black leather boots and a white lace cravat around the neck. The horse furniture, which carries the WR cypher, is white with a scarlet outer line edged with a gold fringe. Colonel Francis Langston had taken command of the regiment on 7 March 1693. *(Anne SK Brown Military Collection, Brown University Library)*

2 – 1st Irish Regiment of Horse, 1751 In 1746 several of the British Army's regiments of horse were re-styled as dragoon guards and with this change the 5th Horse assumed the new title of 1st Irish Horse. Moving on now to 1751 and a warrant issued that year on 1 July regarding cavalry uniform. It was now directed that the 1st Irish Horse should adopt hats ornamented with silver lace and a black cockade, scarlet coats faced with pale blue, the button-holes to be worked with white, and white metal buttons. Waistcoats and breeches were to be pale blue, the red cloaks to be lined with the same colour. The warrant also dealt with horse furniture which was to be pale blue with a border of broad white mohair lace with a scarlet stripe down the centre, and the numeral '1' over the letter 'H' embroidered on a red ground within a wreath of roses and thistles. The new changes are reflected accurately in this signed Richard Simkin watercolour held by the Anne SK Brown Military Collection.

A kettledrummer appears to the left of the image, his blue coat being faced red and heavily adorned with white lace with a red stripe. Traditionally, the colours of drummers' coats at this time were the reverse of those worn by the regiment, in this case light blue with red facings, instead of red with light blue. Unseen in the picture is the drummer's red waistcoat and breeches.

The regiment had been raised by the Earl of Arran in 1685 and became the 4th Royal Irish Dragoon Guards in 1788. *(Image courtesy of the Anne SK Brown Military Collection, Brown University Library)*

3 – 4th Dragoon Guards. 1814 In this watercolour painting by Richard Simkin dated 1814 we see two officers leading a patrol. Both wear the black leather helmet introduced two years earlier, its high gilt crest having a black tuft and a long horsehair main. The gilt plate at the front carried the regimental title and the royal cypher. With blue lines running through broad lace down the front, the scarlet jackets also date from 1812. A crimson sash is being worn round the waist and a white sword-belt is being worn which has a gilt clap. The regiment is easily identified via the embroidery on the horse furniture. Always keen on detail, Richard Simkin has been carful to indicate the men's blue and white girdles worn around the waist. *(Image courtesy of the Anne SK Brown Military Collection, Brown University Library)*

4 – 4th (Royal Irish) Dragoon Guards, Kettledrummer Another of the regiment's kettledrummers, this time as depicted by artist F Stansell for WJ Gordon's 1914 book, *Bands of the British Army*. The change in title to 4th

Dragoon Guards was notified in a General Order dated 14 February 1788, His Majesty the King later confirming the title of 4th (Royal Irish) Regiment of Dragoon Guards on 18 April of the same year. Seen on the blue drum banner are the Crown and Harp badges conferred on the regiment by Queen Victoria in 1838 and the Star of the Order of St Patrick which had been used as a badge by the 1st Irish Horse from 1783. The devices are surrounded by scrolls bearing the regiment's many battle honours.

5 – 4th (Royal Irish) Dragoon Guards Much of the regiment's history is in this Gale & Polden postcard. Produced from artwork supplied by Ernest Ibbetson, the artist has given the nearest rider a Scout's arm badge.

5TH (PRINCESS CHARLOTTE OF WALES'S) DRAGOON GUARDS

TITLES
1685 – Colonel the Duke of Shrewsbury's Regiment of Horse
1687 – 6th Regiment of Horse or 7th Regiment of Horse
1717 – 2nd (or Green) Irish Horse
1788 – 5th Dragoon Guards
1804 – 5th (Princess Charlotte of Wales's) Dragoon Guards

BATTLE HONOURS
'Blenheim', 'Ramillies', 'Oudenarde', 'Malplaquet', 'Beaumont', 'Salamanca', 'Vittoria', 'Toulouse', 'Peninsula', 'Balaclava', 'Sevastopol', 'Defence of Ladysmith', 'South Africa 1899-1902'

RECOMMENDED FURTHER READING
Historical Record of the Fifth, or Princess Charlotte of Wales's Regiment of Dragoon Guards by Richard Cannon and published by Longman, Orme & Co, London, 1839. Contains two colour plates of uniform. Also *The Story of a Regiment of Horse* which was compiled by Major the Hon Ralph Legge Pomeroy taking the history of the regiment from its formation up until 1922. Published in Edinburgh by William Blackwood & Sons in 1924. There are two volumes containing nine colour plates of uniform.

IMAGES
1 – 5th Dragoon Guards, 1705-1839 In this watercolour painting from the Anne SK Brown Military Collection we have a fine example of the uniforms worn by the regiment ranging from 1705 to 1839. Painted in 1881 by Reginald Augustus Wymer (1849-1935), the first image (bottom left) shows a

mounted officer of 1705 who wears a scarlet coat decorated with silver lace across the chest. Large buff gauntlet gloves are being worn with silver buttons and lace. Queen Ann having ascended to the throne in 1702, it is her cypher that we see on the buff horse furniture.

By 1711, records uniform authority WY Carman, the coats of the regiment were red faced with green, and moving on to 1742 (top right) we see green on the cuff and, just visible, on a turnback. As Mr Carman points out, the Earl of Cadogan had become colonel in 1703 and at that time the choice of a regiment's facing colour was most often or not purely at the whim of its commander. After all, he was suppling clothing at his own expense. Certainly, the Earl's coat of arms included a green crest. The image also shows a green flask cord, green breeches and red horse furniture charged with a trophy of arms within silver embroidery.

In the centre of the painting and dated 1794 we have a red coat, this time decorated with gold lace on the collar, lower arm and across the chest in seven rows. A white turnback is visible and, although WY Carman notes that on conversion to dragoon guards in 1788 that yellow facings had replaced the green, Wymer has nonetheless shown green in his watercolour. Green, however, had been permitted once again in March 1800.

Wymer's figure of 1814 shows the black leather helmet of the time with its long flowing black horsehair mane and gilt plate bearing the royal cypher and crown. Green is once again in evidence on the collar, shoulder straps, turnbacks and as a silk line running through the centre of the gold-laced girdle. The artist's last figure, now with the heavily-crested helmet, is dated 1839.

2 – 5th (Princess Charlotte of Wales's) Dragoon Guards, 1828 Published by Samuel William Fores of 41 Piccadilly, London from artwork provided by William Heath (1795-1840) this aquatint shows three officers in the year 1828. A feature here is the regiment's green overalls with their broad gold side stripes. The officer on the right of the image wears the elaborate dress of the time, the uniform worn when attending levees and in the evenings. A cocked hat was chosen for such an occasion as it neatly folded flat when removed and could conveniently be carried under the arm. The heavy helmet, with its large black plume, would have posed a far greater problem. The hat has flowing red and white feathers and gold bullion tassels at each corner. Also note the regimental green, just visible among the heavy gold-laced collar and cuffs and as edging to the gold sword-belt.

3 – Major John Wallace King Signed and dated Nel Carter 1847, this original watercolour painting of Major John Wallace King who joined the regiment as a cornet in 1825. His commission was dated 24 March. His promotion to lieutenant was on 14 February 1828, as captain on 29 December 1832 and major, 14 March 1845. *(Image courtesy of the Anne SK Brown Military Collection, Brown University Library)*

4 – A Sentry of the 5th Dragoon Guards at Bulford Camp Bulford Camp on Salisbury Plain in Wiltshire was set up by the British Army in 1897. Originally an area of tents and huts close to Bulford village, the camp was later extended to include permanent barracks, churches and even schools for the children of resident soldiers. Georges Scott's 'Studies of the British Army at Bulford Camp' featuring a sentry of the 5th Dragoon Guards was published as a supplement to *The Graphic* on 26 October 1901 and, as the caption informs, was 'drawn from life.' Georges Scott was born in France on 10 June 1873 and was a noted war correspondent and illustrator for the French magazine *L'Illustration*.

In this 11¼ x 9¼ study we see scores of tents filling the hillside, the artist placing suggestions of men and horses which give a hint as to the busyness of the place. Pegging its way down the slope comes the canvas, ending with one tent, the occupier of which sits on a wooden bench outside enjoying a pipe and a chat with a sergeant. In blue uniform, we can just make out the rampant lion NCO's arm badge of the 7th Dragoon Guards. Welcome in bad weather must have been the wooden hut just visible on the right of the image. Wearing a brass helmet with star plate displaying in its centre the numeral '5', the main feature of the painting stands at ease, his carbine at his side. A white leather pouch-belt is being worn over a scarlet, five-button frock jacket which has a dark blue collar and steel shoulder chains. Normally the regiment's distinctive white-over-red plume, which had replaced the black type in 1855, would be worn from the spike at the top of the helmet, but these were removed during camp.

5 – 5th Dragoon Guards Chromolith by George Berridge & Co of 179-180 Upper Thames Street, London after Richard Simkin showing an officer of the regiment around 1888. The image was published as a supplement to the *Army and Navy Gazette* on 4 August 1888.

6th Dragoon Guards (Carabiniers)

Titles
1685 – Queen Dowager's Regiment of Horse
1690 – 8th Regiment of Horse, also 9th
1692 – King's Carabiniers
1743 – 3rd Irish Horse
1788 – 6th Dragoon Guards (Carabiniers)

Battle Honours
'Blenheim', 'Ramillies', 'Oudenarde', 'Malplaquet', 'Warburg', 'Willems', 'Sevastopol', 'Delhi 1857', 'Afghanistan 1879-80', 'Relief of Kimberley', 'Paardeberg', 'South Africa 1899-1902'

Recommended Further Reading
Historical Record of the Sixth Regiment of Dragoon Guards, or Carabineers by Richard Cannon and published in London by Longman, Orme & Co in 1839. Contains three coloured plates of uniform. A continuation of this history was published in 1888 by Gale & Polden. Note: Carabineers was an alternative and early spelling of the title.

Images
1 – 3rd Irish Horse Richard Cannon records that the regiment's first uniform was scarlet with sea green facings, a colour which he suggests was a favourite of Queen Catherine. He also mentions that, having made an appearance on Hounslow Heath before the king, '…the Queen Dowager's troopers exhibited sea-green ribands in their broad-brimmed hats, and the officers displayed ostrich feathers; both officers and troopers ornamented the heads and tails of their horses with sea-green ribands, and their waistcoats, breeches, and embroidered horse furniture were of the same colour.' The writer also mentions that each troop was in possession of standards of sea green silk ornamented with regimental devices. At this time, the men were wearing steel cuirassiers.

After the death of Queen Anne, and the accession of King George I in 1714, the regiment's sea green facings were changed to a pale yellow. This colour can be seen in this unsigned watercolour held at the Anne SK Brown Military Collection. Painted sometime after 1743, the trooper wears a scarlet coat with long tails, yellow appearing on the collar, forming wide lapels, the cuffs and turnbacks. His breeches are yellow, and his rolled cloak shows a yellow lining. The horse furniture is also yellow, with white and blue braid, and has been embroidered with the royal cypher and the number 'III' on a red ground within the centre of a union wreath. Wide buff belts are worn, one of which has a metal hook attached to carbine which rests in a leather bucket. The artist has shown the man wearing a cuirass under his coat. *(Image courtesy of the Anne SK Brown Military Collection. Brown University Library)*

2 – 6th Dragoon Guards Artist Richard Caton Woodville dates this original watercolour of an officer as 1844. He shows the gilt heavy dragoon helmet with its long flowing horsehair mane and the white facings that had been ordered via a Royal Warrant of December 1767. We can see this clearly on the collar, the turnbacks and the sabretache which has gold lace and the royal cypher, 'VR'. Heavy gold bullion epaulets are being worn, Dress Regulation at the time directing that these were decorated with regimental badges. The flowing waist sash of crimson and gold has mixed red and gold tassels.

The horse furniture includes a black sheep-skin edged with scarlet, and a '…shabraque of blue cloth; square corners, embroidered with regimental device, and trimmed with gold lace. Double border of gold lace…the outer row an inch and three quarters, the inner one inch wide.' That description from Dress Regulations mentions a regimental device which in this case was crossed carbines. They are just visible below the sash tassels.

Richard Caton Woodville has provided us with a detailed rear view of the officers dress and equipment. Clearly seen are the white turnback with gold lace edging, and the three gilt buttons on each side of the tails. The pouch-belt and pouch are clear too, the description in Dress Regulations giving: 'Morocco leather, colour of regimental facing; back and front covered with velvet or cloth of the same colour; the flap five inches and three quarters wide at top, and six inches and three quarters at bottom; six inches deep; a gold half-inch lace round the

edges, showing a light of the velvet or cloth on the outward edges; gold embroidered V.R., surmounted by a crown relieved in silver, and encircled with oak leaves.' Note how the shabraque is held in place via a loop through which passes the horse's tail. *(Image courtesy of the Anne SK Brown Military Collection, Brown University Library)*

3 – 6th Carabineers, 1828 Engraved by and after William Heath (1785-1840), this image shows a single-breasted scarlet coat with nine buttons in the front, each with two loops of silver lace. The coat tails, cuffs and collar are decorated in the same way. The helmet has ornamental scrolls, a brass crest and large bear-skin running from the base of the headdress and across the top. The scarlet shabraque is laced all around with crowned 'GR' cypher at the rear.

4 – Reminiscences of the Camp Featuring officers of the 6th Dragoon Guards, this lithograph of 1853 produced by Vincent Brooks after Henry Alken (1785-1851) hold much detail. With tents all around and a black dog providing an audience, members of the band practise. Just to their left two men in white stable jackets, one with a saddle over his shoulder, stop for a chat. Others dressed the same are busy preparing forage for the horses. Inside the nearest tent, an officer wearing a white shirt shaves, while outside another, already up and dressed, relaxes on a campaign chair and catches up with the latest news. The men are now dressed in blue, still with their old white facings. One wears a stable jacket which is single-breasted, edged with gold lace, the collar rounded in front, the cuffs two inches deep at the back seam, and three inches at the front. The shoulders have plain gold cord with a small regimental button. Blue cloth forge caps are worn with a one-inch-and-three-quarters-wide gold band and gold Russia braid decoration. *(Image courtesy of the Anne SK Brown Military Collection, Brown University Library)*

5 - Ready For Inspection, 6th Dragoon Guards (Carabineers) 'Ready For Inspection, 6th Dragoon Guards, (Carabineers),' Frederick Stansell's caption leads the eye to eighteen mounted cavalrymen paraded in two ranks on grass. Swords are drawn by the two officers at the front, the rank and file behind holding lances by their side. In *Richard Simkin's Uniforms of the British Army, The Cavalry Regiment*, WY Carman points out that the carrying of lances in the front ranks of heavy cavalry during modern warfare [c 1903] was an idea that did not turn out to be practical— a new pattern of sword having been issued, it was found that a dragoon with this weapon could reach further than the lance. Dark blue uniforms with white facings identify the regiment. The title 'King's Carabiniers' was conferred on the regiment in 1692 shortly after the regiment had been armed with what was commonly referred to at the time as 'short pistols.' Here on the white, edged with gold, shabraque of the officers' mounts, the regiment's crossed carbines are clearly seen. The image is from *Soldiers of the King* by Frederick Stansell.

7TH (THE PRINCESS ROYAL'S) DRAGOON GUARDS

TITLES
1688 – Colonel the Earl of Devonshire's Regiment of Horse, also known as 10th Horse
1690 – Schomberg's Horse
1691 – 8th Horse
1720 – Colonel (afterwards Earl) Ligonier's (the English) Horse
1749 – 4th (or Black) Irish Horse
1788 – 7th (The Princess Royal's) Dragoon Guards

BATTLE HONOURS
'Blenheim', 'Ramillies', 'Oudenarde', 'Malplaquet', 'Dettingen', 'Warburg', 'South Africa 1848-7', 'Tel-el-Kabir', 'Egypt 1882', 'South Africa 1900-02'

RECOMMENDED FURTHER READING
Historical Record of the Seventh, or Princess Royal's Regiment of Dragoon Guards by Richard Cannon and published in London

by Longman, Orme & Co in 1839. Contains two colour plates of uniform. Colonel CW Thompson's *Seventh (Princess Royal's) Dragoon Guards* covers the history of the regiment from its formation in 1688 until 1882.

IMAGES

1 – 7th Dragoon Guards, 1828 It is thought that the Earl of Devonshire had provided the regiment with dark blue coats lined with white flannel, the choice of the former colour having been influenced by his heraldry. By 1690, however, red coats were being worn by Schomberg's Horse. The *Clothing* book of 1742 gives a red coat with black facings, the artist Richard Simkin later producing a painting of an officer which also showed buff linings to the coat, together with gold lace on the hat. The horse furniture was also buff and carried a trophy of arms as decoration. For a figure dated 1751, the regiment now the 4th Irish Horse, David Morier painted a mounted trooper, now in the Royal Collection, wearing a scarlet coat with black cuffs and black lapels that reached down to the lowest part of the garment. A buff waistcoat is clearly visible, the turnbacks being of the same colour. The buff horse furniture has a white edging with a narrow black stripe running through the centre.

Painting an officer of 1828 (illustrated) Richard Simkin gives him the blackened-brass Roman-style helmet with its gilt fittings and high black bearskin crest. The scarlet single-breasted coat is decorated at the front with pairs of lace loops around the gilt buttons and has a similar arrangement on the lower arms running up from the black cuffs. Gold covers almost the entire area of the collar, black being just visible at the back. The epaulettes are of gold bullion, the pouch-belt two inches and a half wide with central black stripe. This matches the sword-belt which is fastened at the front by a plate bearing the royal cypher surmounted by a crown and encircled by oak leaves. *(Image courtesy of the Anne SK Brown Military Collection, Brown University Library)*

2 – 7th Dragoon Guards, 1827 Drawn, engraved and published by William Heath of No1 Manor Grove, King's Road, Chelsea, this image shows an officer enjoying the hospitality of a young woman wearing a white apron over a red dress. The artist has set his scene in some village or other. Cannon tells us that in January 1827 the regiment was stationed at Newbridge Barracks, Ireland from where it moved to Dublin and quarters in Portobello Barracks. Before the year was out, the 7th Dragoon Guards had transferred to Liverpool in April, from where it marched to Coventry and Birmingham. Here it remained until the following spring. *(Image courtesy of the Anne SK Brown Military Collection, Brown University Library)*

3 – 7th Dragoon Guards, c1909 The Anne SK Brown Military Collection is fortunate in having many of the original watercolour paintings that were used in the production of postcard sets published by the Aldershot firm of Gale & Polden. In this study by Ernest Ibbetson a sergeant looks back down a dusty

lane after his men have passed through. A soldier of long experience, his two medals tell us that he had served in the Second Boer War, the one on the left being the Queen's Medal awarded for that campaign, the other that issued after Victoria's death and bearing the head of King Edward VII. The 7th Dragoon Guards has sailed for South Africa on 8 February 1900, arriving onboard the *Armenian* at the Cape on 1 March. The regiment did much good work throughout the war, Lord Kitchener in his despatch of 8 August 1901 mentioning that, 'At midnight on 30th July Colonel Lowe [Lieutenant-Colonel William Henry Muir Lowe], 7th Dragoon Guards, successfully surprised a farmhouse, from which he took 11 armed prisoners, with rifles, bandoliers, and horses.' John Stirling, in his book *Our Regiments in South Africa 1899-1902*, notes that 'It was these useful captures and constant night attacks which were to worry the enemy into ending the campaign.'

The sergeant's helmet has the figure 7 in the centre of a star plate, the plume now being of a black and white mixture. On the collar, and worn above his chevrons, is the regimental white metal badge of a demi-lion issuant from a coronet. This, the crest of Sir John Louis Ligonier, 1st Earl Ligonier who had become colonel of the regiment in 1720. *(Image courtesy of the Anne SK Brown Military Collection, Brown University Library)*

4 – Kettledrummer, c1903 Simple, but striking design for the drum banner. In deep blue, the royal arms are shown surmounted by a princess's coronet with below on a triple scroll, The Princess Royal's Dragoon Guards. On either side, a laurel spray. Interestingly, the banner is dark blue and not, as would be expected, the black of the regiment's facing colour.

In his comprehensive articles on drum horses and banners (*Bulletin of the Military Historical Society* during the 1960s) Mr RG Harris draws our attention to the wearing by the kettledrummer of brass shoulder scales, '…an article of dress that went out in the 1850s'. A photograph taken most probably just after the South Africa War, notes RG Harris, 'shows the shoulder scales still in use….' Image No 4 is from Gordon's *Bands of the British Army*, the artist

Frederick Stansell using the photograph mentioned for his painting.

5 – Kettledrummer, c1906 Mr RG Harris in the article mentioned above refers to a postcard produced about 1906 by Gale & Polden. Originally a photograph, the item is illustrated here and shows that the helmet plume has now been changed from the white shown in Image 4 to black and white. Also note that there are no brass shoulder scales in evidence and that the picture shows a blue (or is it black?) shabraque edged gold with the Garter and the number 7 above DG. Mr Harris referes to the latter as a 'special' pattern, then goes on to say, 'Strangely enough this appears to be the only illustration in which a shabraque is shown and one cannot help but wonder whether it has not actually been superimposed.'

1st (Royal) Dragoons

Titles
1661 – Tangier Horse
1683 – King's Own Royal Regiment of Dragoons
1690 – Royal Regiment of Dragoons
1751 – 1st (Royal) Dragoons

Battle Honours
'Tangier 1662-80', 'Dettingen', 'Warburg', 'Beaumont', 'Willems', 'Fuentes d'Onor', 'Peninsular', 'Waterloo', 'Balaklava', 'Sevastopol', 'Relief of Ladysmith', 'South Africa 1899-1902'

Recommended Further Reading
Historical Records of the First, or The Royal Regiment of Dragoons by Richard Cannon and published in London by Longman, Orme & Co in 1840. Contains two colour plates of uniform. With eight fine colour plates, General De Ainslie's *Historical Record of the First or the Royal Regiment of Dragoons* which was published in 1887 by the London firm of Chapman & Hall. A first class reference which covers the regiment's history from formation up until 1886. The artist un-named, but possibly the work of Richard Simkin, five of the colour plates are illustrated below.

Images

1 – 1st Royal Dragoons, 1660 General de Ainslie records how the Earl of Peterborough's Troop of Horse in the autumn of the following year had mustered in St George's Fields, Southwark, many in the ranks being veterans of the Civil War. The author also notes that the men were armed with cuirasses, iron headpieces called potts, long swords and a pair of large pistols. High boots reaching to the middle of the thigh were worn with scarlet vests. Regarding the officers' dress, the general notes how hats were worn which were 'decorated with a profusion of feathers.' Both officers and men are on record as having 'ornamented' their horses' heads and tails with large bunches of ribbons, as can be seen in Richard Simkin's painting. The Earl of Peterborough's troop was designated as the Tangier Horse and as such fought against the Moors during the British occupation of Tangiers from 1662 to 1684. From *Historical Records of the First or The Royal Regiment of Dragoons* by General de Ainslie, published by Chapman & Hall, London, 1887. Plate by Vincent Brooks Day & Son after Richard Simkin.

2 – 1st Royal Dragoons, 1742 This colour plate is dated 1742, the artist having drawn his reference from the *Clothing* book of that year. Here we have a red coat and breeches, blue cuffs, collar patch and turn backs on the skirts. There are yellow or gold buttonhole loops decorating the front of the coat, the flask cord on the buff pouch-belt worn over the left shoulder being blue to match the facings. In November 1741, the Royal Dragoons had moved from Leicestershire to Somersetshire '…and when in the summer of 1742', records General de Ainslie, 'King George II sent 16,000 men into Flanders under Field-Marshal the Earl of Stair, for the purpose of assisting Austria against France, Bavaria, and Prussia, the regiment was selected for this service, and after being reviewed by his Majesty on Hounslow Heath, they embarked in August.' From *Historical Records of the First or The Royal Regiment of Dragoons* by General de Ainslie, published by Chapman & Hall, London, 1887. Plate by Vincent Brooks Day & Son after Richard Simkin.

3 – 1st Royal Dragoons, 1751 In 1751 a regulation was issued regarding clothing extracts from which are included in General de Ainslie's book: '*Coats*—Scarlet, double-breasted, without lapels, lined with blue; the button holes worked with narrow yellow lace, the buttons of yellow metal, set on two and two; a long slash pocket in each skirt; and a yellow worsted aiguillette on the right shoulder. *Waistcoats and breeches*—Blue. *Hats*—Bound with gold lace, and ornamented with a yellow metal loop, and black cockade. *Boots*—Of jacked leather.' Richard Simkin's illustration follow closely these instructions and includes broad, brown leather shoulder and waist belts. From *Historical Records of the First or The Royal Regiment of Dragoons* by General de Ainslie, published by Chapman & Hall, London, 1887. Plate by Vincent Brooks Day & Son after Richard Simkin.

4 – 1st Royal Dragoons, 1809 This year saw the regiment stationed in Ireland where orders were received in August to embark at Cork for Portugal. Having moved into barracks at Belem, a letter complimenting the regiment on its appearance was received by Lieutenant-General Payne (commanding the cavalry) from Lieutenant-General Viscount Wellington. General de Ainslie includes the following extract in his book: 'I arrived here yesterday, and I saw the Royal Dragoons in the streets, and I think that in my life I have never seen a finer regiment…' Here in the 1809 illustration we see two figures, one mounted, the other on foot. From *Historical Records of the First or The Royal Regiment of Dragoons* by General de Ainslie, published by Chapman & Hall, London, 1887. Plate by Vincent Brooks Day & Son after Richard Simkin.

5 – 1st Royal Dragoons, 1815 Here we see the regiment at the time of Waterloo. Having reached a position in front of Waterloo, the regiment passed the night in open fields without provisions of any kind and exposed to continued rain. On the 18th, Captain Charles E Radclyffe of the 1st Dragoons wrote, 'We found ourselves in our place in close column behind the second line of infantry, fetlock deep in mud; no baggage for the officers, and neither provision nor water for the men.' He also mentions how when the regiment went into action: 'every man was wet to the skin.' The regiment's involvement at Waterloo, which included the taking of the Eagle of the French 105th Regiment by Captain Kennedy Clark, has been well documented. General de Ainslie provides the following casualty figures: ninety-seven killed, the same number wounded. More than 150 horses were also lost. From *Historical Records of the First or The Royal Regiment of Dragoons* by General de Ainslie, published by Chapman & Hall, London, 1887. Plate by Vincent Brooks Day & Son after Richard Simkin.

6 – 1st Royal Dragoons, Charge, 1st Royal Dragoons, Review Order In 'Cavalry Charge, 1st Royal Dragoons, Review Order' Frederick Stansell has given the troopers lances. The carrying of lances in the front ranks of cavalry during modern warfare [c 1903] was an idea that did not turn out to be practical—a new pattern of sword having been issued, it was found that a dragoon with this weapon could reach further than the lance, that later to be subsequently discarded by all except the Lancer regiments of course. The artist has done much to show the power of a cavalry charge, both men and horses desperate to reach the scene of the action. See how the black helmet plumes have caught the force of the wind, and the officer's empty scabbard which has been carried from the side up to a point where it hangs horizontally in the air, its occupant now raised high towards the sky. The plate is from *Soldiers of the King*, which was written and illustrated by Frederick Stansell.

2nd Dragoons (Royal Scots Greys)

Titles
1768 – Royal Regiment of Scots Dragoons
1707 – Royal Regiment of North British Dragoons
1751 – 2nd or Royal North British Dragoons
1866 – 2nd Royal North British Dragoons (Scots Greys)
1877 – 2nd Dragoons (Royal Scots Greys)

Battle Honours
'Blenheim', 'Ramillies', 'Oudenarde', 'Malplaquet', 'Dettingen', 'Warburg', 'Willems', 'Waterloo', 'Balaclava', 'Sevastopol', 'Relief of Kimberley', 'Paardeberg', 'South Africa 1899-1902'

Recommended Further Reading
Historical Record of the Royal Regiment of Scots Dragoons now The Second or Royal North British Dragoons, Commonly Called The Scots Greys by Richard Cannon and published in London by Longman, Orme & Co in 1840. Contains one colour plate of uniform. History of the 2nd Dragoons – The Royal Scots Greys, 1678-1893 by Lieutenant-Colonel Percy Groves, published by the Edinburgh firm of W & AK Johnstone in 1893. A thirty-page book with the briefest of regimental histories, but recommended for its four large colour plates after Harry Payne.

Images
1 – 2nd Dragoons, 1706-1864 From *History of the 2nd Dragoons – The Royal Scots Greys* by Lieutenant-Colonel Percy Groves, illustrations by Harry Payne. At the top of this busy colour plate we have an officer of 1831 flanked on either side by Guidons, while moving down the left side there is a mounted private of 1850 and the head and shoulders of another wearing an undress cap with its zig-zag-pattern white lace. On the right there is a mounted private, rear view this time, of 1864 and below him, a representation of a badge. Moving to the bottom of the image we find an officer who is shown leading the charge at Balaclava on 25 October 1854. To the right and left are representations of the Eagle of the 45th French Infantry which was captured at Waterloo by Sergeant Charles Ewart.

Looking as though it had been stuck on separately as an afterthought, the image in the centre of image 5 is of a smooth-faced mounted private with sword drawn and carried over the right shoulder. Harry Payne had, according to a note accompanying the picture, based his work on a sketch that had appeared in 'Remarkable Portraits'. Remarkable indeed it is, as the subject in question is none other than *Mrs* Christian Davies.

In his book, Colonel Groves recalls 'We have no record of the casualties of the Scots Greys at Ramilies, except that amongst their wounded was the "woman-trooper," Mrs Christian Davies, who had served some four years in the regiment without her sex being discovered.'

Christian had married a waiter, one Thomas Welch, who just before the birth of the couple's third child, disappeared. It was later discovered that Welch had enlisted in the army and was then serving overseas with his regiment. Hot on his heels, the deserted wife put on men's clothing and as Christopher Welch herself joined up and was subsequently shipped off to Holland. The record of service that followed would not disgrace any man. Colonel Groves takes up the story: 'At the battle of Landen she was wounded in the ankle, and during the following summer was taken prisoner by the French, but was shortly afterwards exchanged.' After seriously wounding a sergeant who had abused a girlfriend of Christian, she was discharged from her regiment—Lord Orkney's. 'Mrs Welch', (Groves again) 'was, however, so enamoured with military life that she immediately re-enlisted in the Scots Greys.'

Wounded again, this time at Schellenburg, Christian later while guarding prisoners recognised her illusive husband who was then serving with the 1st Regiment of Foot. The couple did not immediately reunite, but for the time being went their separate

ways. The story approaches an end with Mrs Welch's sex being discovered by a surgeon after being treated for yet another wound received in battle. Having got back with her husband, Mr Welch, however, would later be killed in action. Christian married again, this time to a grenadier, Hugh Jones, but he too would be killed in action. Back in England, and as Mrs Davies, she accompanied her new husband into Chelsea Hospital where she died on 7 July 1739.

2 – 2nd Royal North British Dragoons (Scots Greys) on the Line of March. 1743 As the column turns into a muddy country lane, the two leading dragoons are deep in conversation. An officer wearing a crimson sash falling down to his right hip from his shoulder rides to the left of the picture. His trumpeter, as always, is close by and awaiting orders. 'Early in 1743', records Colonel Groves in his *History of the 2nd Dragoons The Royal Scots Greys 1678-1893*, 'the Greys commenced their march for Germany, and were afterwards employed in military operations in Franconia and on the Upper Maine.' 'Lord Stair whose command now numbered some 40,000 men of all arms,' continues Colonel Groves, 'had taken up a position at Hochst, between Metz and Frankfort, when the French general, Marshall Noailles, seized upon the principle fords on the Upper and Lower Maine, thereby cutting off Lord Stair, not only from his anticipated supplies in Franconia, but also from the magazines and stores at Hanau.' In the actions that followed, Colonel Groves noted of the 2nd Dragoons that, 'Their grey horses and grenadier caps rendered them conspicuous.'

3 – A Charge of the 2nd Dragoons (Royal Scots Greys) No doubt inspired by Lady Butler's 'Scotland

Forever' painting, in which the artist depicted the Royal Scots Greys during a charge at the Battle of Waterloo in 1815, Richard Simkin's Victorian full-page image of the regiment shows a similar, but less vibrant scene. Here a trumpeter sounds the 'charge', his scarlet plume distinguishing him from the rest of the regiment who have white. He has crimson and yellow aiguillette cords and, of course, wears the bearskin headdress of the 2nd Dragoons which is unique among British cavalry regiments. A brass fused grenade badge acts as a plume holder which has on the ball the Royal Arms, St Andrew's cross, sprays of rose, thistle and shamrock and the battle honour 'Waterloo'. Unseen in the image, but certainly worth mentioning, is the white metal White Horse of Hanover badge worn on the back of the caps. The facings are blue, the horses, of course, grey. Regarding the trumpeter: trumpets are used by cavalry regiments when dismounted, the smaller bugle, as seen in the illustration, replacing the larger instrument when mounted.

Image from *Our Armies*, illustrated and described by Richard Simkin, with litho work produced in Holland by Emrik & Binger of 21 Berners Street, London. Published by Day & Son, 21A Berners Street and W & Simkin, Marshall, Hamilton, Kent & Co, Ltd in 1890.

4 – Trumpeters in Review Order In this postcard after Harry Payne we see the distinctive scarlet plumes of the regiment's trumpeters. Also unique among British cavalry is the White Horse badge worn at the back of the fur cap. Here too on the collar is an eagle commemorating the capture at Waterloo of the Eagle of the French 45th Regiment.

3rd (King's Own) Hussars

Titles
1685 – Queen Consort's Own Regiment of Dragoons
1692 – Queen's Dragoons
1714 – King's Own Regiment of Dragoons
1751 – 3rd (King's Own) Dragoons
1818 – 3rd (King's Own) Light Dragoons
1861 – 3rd (King's Own) Hussars

Battle Honours
'Dettingen', 'Salamanca', 'Vittoria', 'Toulouse', 'Peninsula', 'Cabool 1842', 'Moodkee', 'Ferozeshah', 'Sobraon', 'Chillianwallah', 'Goojerat', 'Punjaub', 'South Africa 1902'

Recommended Further Reading
Historical Records of the Third, or The King's Own Regiment of Light Dragoons by Richard Cannon and published in London by Parker, Furnivall & Parker in 1847. Contains two colour plates of uniform. A revised edition of Cannon's work was produced in 1857 by Captain George EF Kauntze which has four colour plates and another in 1903 published by WP Griffith & Sons with eight plates.

Images
1 – The Queen Consort's Regiment of Dragoons, 1685 In this hand-coloured aquatint from the Anne SK Brown Military Collection we see an example of the first uniform worn by the regiment. Richard Cannon explains

how, to oppose Monmouth's rebellion '…a number of young men from Berkshire, Middlesex, Herts and Essex were formed into five independent troops of Dragoons.' It was these, together with a number of other troops raised by the king against Monmouth, that would be formed into a regiment with the title of Queen Consort's Regiment of Dragoons.

Engraved by H Barnett, the image shows a mounted soldier with others descending down a slope. Long pikes and banners are in evidence, the men all wearing scarlet cloaks with blue collars. The main feature of the picture wears a scarlet coat which has a blue collar with silver buttons attached. The straight cuffs are also blue, as is the lace around the edge of the garment and between the shoulder and upper arm. A black felt hat with white feather slopes to the right of the wearers head, who has been given brown hair and a short moustache. The sword-belt has an oval device and the horse furniture is blue with a wide yellow strip of lace edged with scarlet. *(Image courtesy of the Anne SK Brown Military Collection, Brown University Library)*

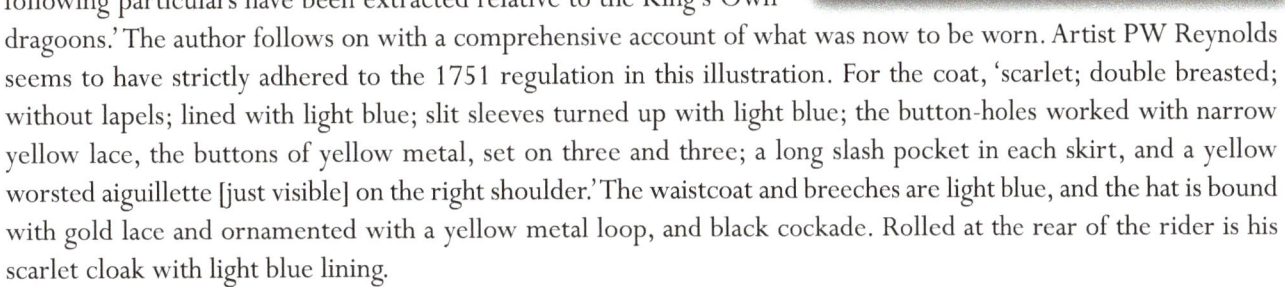

2 – Queen Consort's Own Regiment of Dragoons, c1700
Moving on some fifteen years and to an original watercolour from PW Reynolds. Here we see a long scarlet coat with blue cuffs and turnbacks. The breeches are blue also, as is a long waistcoat which is just visible. Brown leather equipment is being worn, a large pouch supported by a narrow strap across the left shoulder, a smaller one attached to the sword and bayonet belt around the waist. The soft black hat has white braid around the outer edge. *(Image courtesy of the Anne SK Brown Military Collection, Brown University Library)*

3 – 3rd (King's Own) Dragoons, 1751 Richard Cannon records that 'A regulation was issued on the 1st July, 1751 relative to the clothing and standards of the several regiments: from which the following particulars have been extracted relative to the King's Own dragoons.' The author follows on with a comprehensive account of what was now to be worn. Artist PW Reynolds seems to have strictly adhered to the 1751 regulation in this illustration. For the coat, 'scarlet; double breasted; without lapels; lined with light blue; slit sleeves turned up with light blue; the button-holes worked with narrow yellow lace, the buttons of yellow metal, set on three and three; a long slash pocket in each skirt, and a yellow worsted aiguillette [just visible] on the right shoulder.' The waistcoat and breeches are light blue, and the hat is bound with gold lace and ornamented with a yellow metal loop, and black cockade. Rolled at the rear of the rider is his scarlet cloak with light blue lining.

Turning to the horse furniture: PW Reynolds shows a light blue shabraque edged with two lines of yellow lace and with III over D embroidered in yellow on a scarlet ground, all within a circular wreath. The holster cap is of the same blue, its yellow lace having III D in silver on the lower edge, and with a crowned GR cypher. Note how the buff leather shoulder-belt passes through the scarlet strap to secure the musket via a brass hook on the right side. *(Image courtesy of the Anne SK Brown Military Collection, Brown University Library)*

4 – 3rd (King's Own) Light Dragoons, c1851 Moving on from the image above by one hundred years, we now

3

4

have one of the large (approximately twenty by sixteen inches) plates produced by Rudolf Ackermann. Drawn by Henry Martens and engraved by John Harris, this image of the 3rd (King's Own) Light Dragoons was published on 21 June 1851 and shows the regiment now in all dark blue uniforms with scarlet facings. Blue had been reintroduced in 1840. The headdress is different too, it now being a chaco with parallel sides and a Maltese cross device at the front. Seen white in the image, the plume was, according to Dress Regulations, white and black. The dark blue horse furniture and sabretache clearly show the regiment's ancient White Horse of Hanover device.

5

6

5 – 3rd (King's Own) Light Dragoons, 1857 In this original watercolour by Richard Simkin held at the Anne SK Brown Military Collection, we see a different type of chaco to that being worn in the Ackermann print above. Details from Dress Regulations are: 'chaco body, covered with Paris velvet; height, front, five and a quarter inches; sides, six and three-eighths inches; back, nine and one-eighth inches, patent leather sunk top, one inch and one-eighth less in diameter than size of head; patent leather five-eighths of an inch band round bottom of cap, gold inch-and-three-quarters oak band round top of cap; nearly horizontal patent leather three-quarters of an inch gold embroidered peak projecting two-and-a-quarter inches; burnished gilt plain chain three-quarters of an inch wide, with rose ornaments each side of chaco, gilt lion head with ring immediately below gold band at back of chaco; also gilt hook to fasten up chain, front ornament, gilt and silver Maltese cross, with crown above.' A gilt plume socket held the black and white hair plume.

6 – 3rd (King's Own) Hussars, c1909 Showing the familiar Hussar-type fur busby is the original watercolour artwork produced by Ernest Ibbetson for one of Gale & Polden's postcard sets. The old light blue worn by the regiment has been permitted for the busby bag. Just visible above the chevrons of the mounted sergeant is the White Horse arm badge worn by non-commissioned officers. *(Image courtesy of the Anne SK Brown Military Collection, Brown University Library)*

4TH (QUEEN'S OWN) HUSSARS

TITLES
1685 – Princess Anne of Denmark's Dragoons
1688 – Known by the name of colonel
1751 – 4th Dragoons
1788 – 4th or Queen's Own Dragoons
1818 – 4th (Queen's Own) Light Dragoons
1861 – 4th (Queen's Own) Hussars

BATTLE HONOURS
'Dettingen', 'Talavera', 'Albuhera', 'Salamanca', 'Vittoria', 'Toulouse', 'Peninsula', 'Ghuznee 1838', 'Affghanistan 1839', 'Alma', 'Balaklava', 'Inkerman', 'Sevastopol'

RECOMMENDED FURTHER READING
Historical Record of the Fourth, or The Queen's Own Regiment of Light Dragoons, by Richard Cannon and published in London by John W Parker, 1843. Contains one colour plate of uniform. Taking the regiment's history from its formation in 1685 through to 1958 is David Scott Daniell's *4th Hussar, the Story of a British Cavalry Regiment* which was published in 1959 by the Aldershot firm of Gale and Polden. Contains eleven colour portrait and uniform plates.

IMAGES
1 – Sir Robert Rich's Regiment of Dragoons, 1742 Little is known of the early uniform of the Princess Anne of Denmark's Dragoons. In 1686, at a review on Hounslow Heath, the facings of the regiment were noted as 'carnation', but as uniform authority WY Carman points out, this could have been a mistake as drawings made at

2

3

the time of the guidons show yellow. By 1742, however, the *Clothing* book of that year give green.

Sir Robert Rich, member of parliament for St Ives and governor of the Royal Hospital from 1740 until 1768, became colonel in May 1735. Here in the illustration we see a member of his regiment in the form of an original watercolour by R Simkin. Here are the green facings mentioned in the *Clothing* book, the colour appearing on the collar, cuffs and turnbacks. The breeches are also green, as is the horse furniture. Both the shabraque and holster cap being embroidered with a trophy of arms. The cap and buttonhole lace appear as white. *(Image courtesy of the Anne SK Brown Military Collection, Brown University Library)*

2 – 4th Dragoons, 1751 Also by Richard Simkin, this watercolour shows the white lace arrangement in more detail than his precious painting above. As we can see the coat tails are now revealed, and lace now extends in a greater number of buttonhole lines up the sleeve almost to the elbow. Note how the artist has shown the tails covering the sword.

There has been a change in the horse furniture. Still green, we now have a white edging with a scarlet central line together with the royal cypher and crown. Buff leather gauntlet gloves are being worn, the wide pouch-belt shown passing through the buttoned scarlet strap on the left shoulder. Behind the rider, a rolled scarlet cloak showing its green lining. *(Image courtesy of the Anne SK Brown Military Collection, Brown University Library)*

3 – 4th or Queen's Own Dragoons, 1804 We are indeed grateful to the Anne SK Brown Military Collection for the third illustration, one of a set of three (see images 1 and 2 above) watercolours by Richard Simkin. Dated 1804 by the artist, we can now see that the tricorn hat has now given way to a bicorn sporting a white-over-red plume. The coat is now closed, its tails much shorter and with a white lace edging. We also have pointed shoulder straps with lace, the oval wings being red with an edging of white fringed braid, and much less lace on the arms. Gone is the wide buff shoulder-belt, just one of white leather now, and the green breeches which are now buff. *(Image courtesy of the Anne SK Brown Military Collection, Brown University Library)*

4 – 4th Hussars, 1814-1880 In this original watercolour painting by Reginald Augustus Wymer we have a record of several of the uniforms worn between 1814 and 1880. At bottom right we have, with his back to us, a dragoon of 1814 wearing a scarlet jacket with green collar. The shoulder straps are also green and have white lace edgings. A black helmet with gilt of brass fittings is worn which has a long black horsehair plume running from the protruding front of the crest, down the back some three feet. The girdle is white with two green lines.

With the styling as light dragoons in 1818 came a change to blue uniforms with yellow facings. A black broad-topped shako became the headdress, which was worn with a white-over-red swan's feather by the officers. Trousers were sky blue with two stripes of silver lace. But in 1831 William IV made his wish known that all his army was to be clothed in red coats. Subsequently the 4th Light Dragoons once again appeared in red, keeping at the same time the yellow facings of the blue uniforms.

Bottom left of Wymer's painting we have an officer of 1837, his red coat richly decorated with gold lace. Silver lace in the Regular Army had been ordered to be replaced by gold towards the end of 1821. The broad-topped shako has an all-white plume, a large Maltese cross plate in silver and gilt and gold cord cap lines. Short white gloves were worn by light dragoon regiments which allow us to see the cuffs which were richly decorated with gold lace and cord. Just a year before, the regiment's former green facings, seen here in the painting on the collar, cuffs and belts, had been restored. Blue trousers are worn with a gold stripe, the horse furniture white sheepskin, edged with red and green.

Moving now to 1845 and the figure top right of the picture, we find that once more the uniform is blue. The change had occurred in May 1840 and in consequence permission was given to change the facing colour to scarlet. An all-white plume rises high above the black and gilt shako which has retained its Maltese cross plate. The horse furniture is dark blue with a wide gold edging, as is the sabretache with its VR cypher.

After the Crimean Way one of the many changes to uniform was the replacement of the coatee by a tunic entirely of blue cloth, single-breasted and with the collar two inches high and rounded at the front. Here we see it in Wymer's top left figure which he dates as 1857. On each side of the breast there are five loops of gold chain lace with caps and drops fastening with six gold worked olivets. All around the tunic is more gold chain lace. The headdress, tapering at the top, has a red hair plume instead of the white previously worn and still sports a Maltese cross plate.

Changes would be made to the uniform worn when, in 1861 the regiment ceased to be styled as light dragoons and instead became hussars. Wymer's central figure for 1880 shows a mounted officer wearing the familiar hussar-type black fur busby. The busby-bag is yellow and the tall plume scarlet. One significant change in the tunic is that the breast decoration now takes the form of six rows of gold chain lace. *(Image courtesy of the Anne SK Brown Military Collection, Brown University Library)*

5TH (ROYAL IRISH) LANCERS

TITLES
1689 – Raised and known by name of colonel
1694 – Irish Dragoons, or by name of colonel
1704 – Royal Dragoons of Ireland
1751 – 5th (Royal Irish) Dragoons. Disbanded in 1799
1861 – 5th (Royal Irish) Lancers

BATTLE HONOURS
'Blenheim', 'Ramilles', 'Oudenarde', 'Malplaquet', 'Suakin 1885', 'Defence of Ladysmith', 'South Africa 1899-1902'

RECOMMENDED FURTHER READING
The Historical Records of the Fifth (Royal Irish) Lancers from their Foundation as Wynne's Dragoons in 1689 to the Present Day

by Walter Temple Willcox and published in London by Arthur Doubleday & Co. Ltd in 1908. Included seven colour plates of uniform. Also, *The History of the 5th (Royal Irish) Regiment of Dragoons from 1689 to 1799 afterwards The 5th Royal Irish Lancers from 1858 to 1921* which was written by Colonel JR Harvey and Lieutenant-Colonel HA Cape and published by the Aldershot firm of Gale & Polden in 1923. Includes seven colour plates of uniform.

IMAGES

1 – Royal Dragoons of Ireland and 5th (Royal Irish) Dragoons When raised as Colonel James Wynne's Regiment of Dragoons during the troubles in Ireland, records shown that the regiment was dressed in grey and armed with an assortment of weapons. Writing in his book, *Richard Simkin's Uniforms of the British Army The Cavalry Regiments,* WY Carman goes on to say that in 1691, when in battle, 'the only sign of whom they fought for was a green bough in their hats.' By the time they were fighting on the Continent, however, 'they had become royal and would have had red coats with blue facings.' One other record, an order book dated 1731, makes mention of a quantity of gold lace for the use of sergeants and corporals.

In this painting by Richard Simkin we see three figures, the first showing a soldier of 1742 who wears a scarlet coat with blue collar tabs, cuffs and turnbacks. The waistcoat, with its yellow lace decoration, and breeches are also blue. The equipment is buff leather, the wide pouch-belt passing through the scarlet strap on the left shoulder having a blue flask cord. The black felt hat is trimmed with yellow or gold and has a black bow secured by a button on the left side.

Moving on now to the central figure and the year 1751, we can notice several changes. The blue facings remain, but the officer's lace is now silver, and the waistcoat buff edged down the front, bottom and around the pocket flaps with silver. The buttonhole loops are now grouped in threes and a crimson sash is worn from the right shoulder terminating in a bow on the left side. The third figure in Simkin's painting is similarly dressed, but wears a silver aiguillette on the right shoulder and carries a buff pouch-belt.

2 – 5th (Royal Irish) Lancers Having been disbanded at Chatham on 15 April 1799, it would be no doubt due to the problems in India that the regiment was re-raised at Newbridge, Ireland as the 5th (Royal Irish) Lancers. Artist Richard Simkin painted the regiment in 1875 and would have consulted the currant Dress Regulations for officers as his source: 'Tunic – Blue cloth, double-breasted, with front, collar and cuffs of the regimental facings [scarlet]; the front to be worn buttoned back, except on the march or in bad weather; the cuffs pointed, the collar and cuffs ornamented with inch lace round the top. Two rows of buttons in front, 7 in each row, the rows 8 inches apart at the top, and 4 inches as the waist, where the buttons are flat to go under the girdle; 2 buttons at the waist behind. A flap on back of each skirt, edged with square gold cord, 3 buttons on each flap. A welt of the regimental facings in the sleeve and back seams, down the front, and round the skirts, which are lined with black. Shoulder-straps of gold wire cord, lined with blue. Small button at the top; badges of rank in silver.' The girdle referred to was of gold lace, 2½ inches wide with crimson silk stripes.

We can also turn to Dress Regulations for a detailed description of the lace cap: 'Lancer pattern; 6½ inches high in front, 7 inches at the sides, and 8½ inches at the back; 7 inches square at the top. Skull covered with black patent leather, the upper part and top with cloth of the same colour as the facings. Gold gimp and orris cord across the top and down the angles.' Orris cord, 'A pattern in which gold lace or silver lace is worked, especially one in which the edges are ornamented with conical figures placed at equal distances, with spots between them' (Webster).

Seen in Simkin's painting on the left side of the cap at the front is a gold bullion rosette which carries the royal cypher on green velvet. The gilt three-cornered plate at the front displayed the royal arms below a harp between sprays of shamrock together with several battle honours and the regimental title. The plume, horsehair, 12 inches long and rising 4½ inches above the top of the cap, is green. Encircling the cap once, passing round the body and looped on the left breast, the cap lines are of gold gimp and orris cord. The horse furniture includes a black lambskin edged with red cloth and a shabraque embroidered with the regimental device of a harp and crossed lances.

The dismounted officer wears a blue cloth stable jacket with lace edges all round, including the collar. The trousers have double yellow stripes. He also wears the black undress sabretache with regimental device which was taken into use in 1873. *(Image courtesy of the Anne SK Brown Military Collection, Brown University Library)*

3 – 5th (Royal Irish) Lancers, c1909 – Clearly seen in Ernest Ibbetson's original artwork for one of Gale & Polden's postcard sets are the regiment's Irish harp cap and collar badges. A silver version is also being worn on the chevrons of the sergeant, a privilege of none-commissioned officers. The other lancer has dismounted and holds his lance to his left side. The sergeant has exchanged his full-dress headdress for a blue forage cap with scarlet band and cord, but note how he still wears cap lines. *(Image courtesy of the Anne SK Brown Military Collection, Brown University Library)*

4 – 5th (Royal Irish) Lancers, Sentry – One of the many postcards produced from artwork supplied by Harry Payne by Raphael Tuck & Sons, Ltd. A sentry is featured who has been placed at some side gate or other of a Victorian barracks. Behind him all is silent, save for the footsteps of a khaki figure crossing the square.

6th (Inniskilling) Dragoons

TITLES
1689 – Sir Albert Cunningham's Regiment, then known by the name of successive colonels
1751 – 6th (Inniskilling) Dragoons

BATTLE HONOURS
'Dettingen', 'Warburg', 'Willems', 'Waterloo', 'Balaclava', 'Sevastopol', South Africa 1899-1902'

RECOMMENDED FURTHER READING
Historical Record of the Sixth, or Inniskilling Regiment of Dragoons by Richard Cannon and published in London by Parker, Furnivall & Parker in 1847. Contains three colour plates of uniform. Also *The Inniskilling Dragoons, The Records of an Old Heavy Cavalry Regiment* by Major ES Jackson which was published by the London firm of Arthur L Humphreys in 1909. Includes seven colour plates of uniform.

IMAGES
1 – Earl of Stair's Regiment of Dragoons When formed into a regiment at Inniskilling, Colonel Sir Albert Cunningham's men were at first clothed in grey. Little more is on record for this period save that uniform authority WY Carman, writing in his book '*Richard Simkin's Uniforms of the British Army The Cavalry Regiments,* notes that 'There is a tradition that the iron-grey coats had yellow facings.' The author goes on to say that there is a record that in 1692 an order of material received in Ireland suggested that the officers were wearing crimson cloth coats, their waistcoats being ash-coloured. Mr Carman also mentions how the uniforms of the senior officers were decorated with gold loops, thread and buttons, but the lesser lieutenants and cornets had silver lace and buttons.

Thanks to the 1742 *Clothing* book, artist Richard Simkin was able to paint an accurate image of a private of the now Earl of Stair's Regiment of Dragoons around that time. Sir Albert Cunningham had been killed at the Battle of the Boyne, his immediate successor being Robert Echlin in December 1691. John Dalrymple 2nd Earl of Stair was made colonel in March 1715, but he was replaced in 1734 by Charles Cadogan. He was, however, reappointed on 25 April 1743. The scarlet coat has a yellow patch on the collar, yellow cuffs and skirt turnbacks. The same colour was used for the waistcoat and breeches. The buttons are arranged singularly with white cord or lace, the black hat trimmed with white. One of Cannon's colour plates shows a mounted private for the same period.

2 – Cornet Thomas Mervyn Medlycott, 1792 Richard Cannon devotes almost three pages to the uniform relevant to the 6th Dragoons as directed by a regulation issued in

1751. For the coat we have scarlet, double-breasted and without lapels, 'lined with full yellow; slit sleeves, turned up with full yellow, the button-holes worked with narrow white lace, the buttons white metal, set on two and two, a long slash pocket in each skirt; and a white shoulder-knot, or aiguillette, on the right shoulder.' Waistcoats and breeches were to be of full yellow, the hats bound with silver lace and ornamented with a white metal loop and a black cockade.

Thomas Mervyn Medlycott was born on 25 October 1773, the son of Thomas and Jane Medlycott. He would join the regiment about the time of the illustration, an original watercolour by PW Reynolds which he dates 1792. The image shows the young officer posing with his hat in hand, the yellow of his collar, cuffs and skirt linings bright in the picture. The ten silver buttons down the front of the single-breasted coat are worked with white lace, as are those on the cuffs, turnbacks and waistcoat. Silver epaulettes are being worn and also a gorget inscribed with a representation of Inniskilling Castle between the cypher GR.

At the beginning of 1793, the 6th (Inniskilling) Dragoons was increased to nine troops and held in readiness for foreign service. In Europe the French republicans, records Cannon, were 'pursuing a career of cruelty, spoliation and bloodshed', and having turned their attention elsewhere, they attacked Holland. As a result a British force was sent out, part of which was the 6th Dragoons who left their station at York for Ostend in June 1793. Just nineteen years of age, Cornet Thomas Mervyn Medlycott would die just days after, on 4 July. *(Image courtesy of the Anne SK Brown Military Collection, Brown University Library)*

3 – 6th (Inniskilling) Dragoons, Waterloo, 1815
Richard Simkin's painting shows the regiment in a charge at Waterloo in 1815. The 6th (Inniskilling) Dragoons, along with the 1st and 2nd Dragoons, formed the Union Brigade, the formation being as it were made up of English, Scottish and Irish regiments. On 18 June, at around two in the afternoon, the brigade under General Ponsonby was ordered to charge, a heavy assault being made by the French on the British line. Possibly it was this important move by the cavalry that Richard Simkin had in mind for his painting. As a French soldier lies dead or wounded on the battlefield, on in their scarlet jackets and black flowing helmet manes go the Inniskillings, their castle badge clearly visible on the horse furniture. The Union Brigade smashed their way through the French infantry then made for the enemy's artillery. But the excitement of the charge would cause the cavalrymen to go too far, an error that gave French reinforcements the opportunity to make a counterattack resulting in the death of General Ponsonby. The losses to the Inniskillings: eighty-six officers and men killed with 107 wounded. The horses too would suffer with 164 killed and 207 wounded.

4 – 6th (Inniskilling) Dragoons, c1845 Published by Rudolf Ackermann on 28 July 1845, this print shows the gilt helmet introduced in 1844 and worn until 1849. The flowing black horsehair mane measures some two feet ten

5

6TH INNISKILLING DRAGOONS.

inches in length, terminating in a thistle-shaped brush held in a gold embroidered boss at the front. Gold bullion epaulettes are being worn with the regiment's Inniskilling Castle badge embroidered in silver within the crescent. The trousers are a dark blue with a stripe of gold lace, 1¾ inches wide down the outward seams. The Inniskilling Castle is again seen, this time embroidered in gold on the gold-edged pointed tail of the shabraque. The artist for the work was Henry I Daubrawa, the engraver John Harris.

5 – Kettledrummer From *Bands of the British Army* written by WJ Gordon with illustrations by Frederick Stansell, this study of a kettledrummer and drum horse clearly show the regiment's Inniskilling Castle badge. RG Harris in his superb series of articles for the Military Historical Society dealing with mounted bands and drum horses, tells how a new drum horse had joined the regiment in 1897 which was noted for its exceptionally long flowing white mane. At the same time the drum banners illustrated by Frederick Stansell were introduced as a replacement for those that had been in use since shortly after the Crimean War. Note the kettledrummer's red instead of white plume.

7TH QUEEN'S OWN HUSSARS

TITLES
1690 – Raised and known by colonel's name
1715 – Prince of Wales's Own Royal Dragoons
1727 – Queen's Own Dragoons
1751 – 7th or Queen's Own Dragoons
1783 – 7th or Queen's Own Light Dragoons
1807 – 7th (Queen's Own) Light Dragoons Hussars
1861 – 7th Queen's Own Hussars

BATTLE HONOURS
'Dettingen', 'Warburg', 'Beaumont', 'Willems', 'Orthes', 'Peninsula', 'Waterloo', 'Lucknow', 'South Africa 1901-02'

RECOMMENDED FURTHER READING
Historical Record of the Seventh, or The Queen's Own Regiment of Hussars by Richard Cannon and published in London by John W Parker in 1842. Contains one colour plate of uniform. Also *The 7th (Queen's Own) Hussars*, a two volume set by CRB Barrett and published in London by the Royal United Services Institution in 1914. Includes ten colour plates of uniform.

IMAGES
1 – 7th or Queen's Own Dragoons, 1760 The regiment was raised in Scotland under the command of Colonel

Robert Cunningham from a number of independent troops of horse and dragoons. He was subsequently succeeded by William Kerr, the 2nd Marquess of Lothian in 1690, Patrick Hume, Lord Polwarth in 1707 and the Hon William Kerr on 10 October 1709. Little is known of the early uniform, WY Carman suggesting that it could possibly have been grey, a colour much favoured at the time in Scotland. The *Clothing* book of 1742 shows the Queen's Own Dragoons wearing red coats with collar patches, cuffs, turnbacks, breeches and cloak linings in white. The horse furniture, with its embroidered crown over the Garter, was also white. The c1751 David Morier painting held in the Royal Collection at Windsor, varies in as much as the breeches are shown as scarlet. Regulations at the time, however, give white.

In this original watercolour painted in 1910 by Richard Caton Woodville, we have a mounted private of what in 1760 was titled as the 7th or Queen's Own Dragoons. As a side-on view, clearly shown by the artist is the shoulder knot behind the right shoulder which would have been discontinued four years after the date of the painting in 1764. We can also see the wide buff leather belt and pouch, what looks like the number 7 and letter D just behind, and an example of how the musket was held when mounted in a leather bucket then secured via a metal clip (out of site below the arm) attached to the pouch-belt. The horse furniture has a blue line, the holster-caps being embroidered with the GR Cypher below a crown and in white, 7D. *(Image courtesy of the Anne SK Brown Military Collection, Brown University Library)*

2 – 7th Queen's Own Light Dragoons, 1783 Moving on to 1783 and this superbly detailed portrait of an officer c1783 by Richard Simkin. Now designated as light dragoons, the black leather helmet with its crest and tall white feather has replaced the hat and a turban of red with silver lines is quite clear in the painting. Here we have a scarlet coat with white facings and intricate workings around the buttonholes. A scarlet waistcoat is being worn, this with much simpler lace, and over this a crimson waist sash. WY Carman in his book on Simkin's art marks this image as interesting as the source of the artist's work is not known. He also makes the point that the meticulous history of the regiment written by CRB Barrett makes no mention of such a uniform. However, notes Mr Carman, it is just possible that '…the light dragoon pattern garments were worn in red before 1784 when blue was authorized.'

3 – 7th Hussars, 1820 CRB Barrett's detailed history of the 7th Hussars records how in 1805 the regiment assumed the clothing and appointments of hussars instead of those of light dragoons. Volume 42 (1964) of the *Journal of the Society for Army Historical Research* included a colour plate of Major Edward Hodge which had been taken from an original watercolour signed and dated 'R Dighton June 1805' which shows the officer wearing a tall light blue cylindrical cap with a long blue wing reaching down well below the waist. But soon the more familiar fur busby would come into use and it is this form of headdress that we see in the John Lewis Marks hand-coloured aquatint illustrated.

The artist has provided a background showing members of the regiment galloping out of camp with their swords drawn. In the distance,

two men and a trumpeter stand on a hill by a lone stone structure of three steps. Featured is a mounted soldier who wears a tall black shako decorated with a wide line of yellow lace at the top, yellow cap lines and fittings. The all-blue uniform shows no sign of the regiment's white facing colour save for the edging and cuffs of the pelisse. Yellow almost covers the entire chest, the same colour forming a wide stripe down the outer seam of the blue overalls and the edging to the sabretache and shabraque. The image also includes the address of the artist and publisher, No 17 Artillery Street, Bishopsgate, and its original 3d-for-colour cost. *(Image courtesy of the Anne SK Brown Military Collection, Brown University Library)*

4 – Cornet of the 7th Hussars, c1840-45 Dated some twenty years on from Image No 3, the artist responsible for this original watercolour painting (the Anne SK Brown Military Collection suggest that it might be MH Proste) shows a cornet of the 7th Hussars c1840-45. For a description of what is being worn we turn to *Regulations for the Dress of General Staff And Regimental Officers of the Army* for 1846 which for the jacket gives as being entirely of blue cloth with a Prussian collar full three inches deep, laced round and ornamented with Russia braid which extends the full width of the jacket across the breast terminating in three inches at the bottom. Worn over the left shoulder, the pelisse is also of blue cloth decorated similarly to the jacket with gimp Russia braid, its collar and cuffs edged with fur. On a table by the officers' side, the shako as worn in Image 3. What delights, I wonder, lay within the pages of the large portfolio on the right which is labelled '7th Hussars' and possibly has a name beginning with Joseph (below)? Going on this, the ASK Brown notes that accompany this plate suggest that the subject of the image is perhaps Joseph Hely who was commissioned cornet and riding master in the 7th Hussars on 10 April 1840. *(Image courtesy of the Anne SK Brown Military Collection, Brown University Library)*

5 – 7th The Queen's Own Hussars on Escort Duty – Part of the Anne SK Brown Military Collection, the notes accompanying this image state: 'Original watercolour signed Atkinson; body of hussars, escorting open travelling carriage and wagon with wounded or prisoners on country road, perhaps in Canada (?), man and women watching on the right.' The 7th Hussars were in Canada from 1838 to 1842. *(Image courtesy of the Anne SK Brown Military Collection, Brown University Library)*

8TH (KING'S ROYAL IRISH) HUSSARS

TITLES
1693 – Cunningham's Dragoons, later by the name of successive colonels
1751 – 8th Dragoons
1775 – 8th Light Dragoons
1777 – 8th The (King's Royal Irish) Light Dragoons
1822 – 8th King's Royal Irish (Light) Dragoons (Hussars)
1861 – 8th (King's Royal Irish) Hussars

BATTLE HONOURS
'Leswarree', 'Hindoostan', 'Alma', 'Balaclava', 'Inkerman', 'Sevastopol', 'Central India', 'Afghanistan 1879-80', 'South Africa 1900-02'

RECOMMENDED FURTHER READING
Historical Record of the Eighth or The King's Royal Irish Regiment of Hussars by Richard Cannon, published in London by John W Parker in 1844. Contains two colour plates of uniform. Also, and in two volumes, *The History of the VIII King's Royal Irish Hussars, 1693-1927* which was written by the Rev Robert H Murray and published in 1928 by the Cambridge firm of W Heffer & Sons, Ltd. Contains seven colour plates of uniform.

IMAGES

1 – St George's Regiment of Dragoons The regimental records tell us how this corps had been formed in 1693 from Irish Protestants, its first commander being Colonel Henry Cunningham. The first uniform known to have been worn by Cunningham's Dragoons was scarlet with yellow facings, waistcoats, breeches and horse furniture, its badge the royal cypher and crown. The hats were round with broad brims turned up all around. WY Carman's book, *Richard Simkin's Uniforms of the British Army Cavalry,* includes an image of a private of 1742 in what is now Richard St George's Regiment of Dragoons. He wears a long scarlet coat with yellow facings and what appears to be an orange or light brown waistcoat, the breeches being of the same colour. Richard St George had taken command of the regiment in 1740, WY Carman mentioning how his uniform coat, one of the oldest preserved, was covered with silver embroidery.

Also to record the uniform was the Rev Percy Sumner who shows a private walking his horse along a narrow country track. The artist gives a clear view of the waistcoat which

has white metal buttons and white lace. The coat has scarlet shoulder straps through which wide buff belts pass, and white lace or braid decorating the button holes. Just visible on the right side of the horse is the leather bucket which secures the musket, the bayonet for which is housed when not in use on the private's left side with his sword. *(Image courtesy of the Anne SK Brown Military Collection, Brown University Library)*

2 – 8th King's (King's Royal Irish) Light Dragoons, c1790 In the David Henry Parry original watercolour painting illustrated we see a private of the regiment around 1790. As can be seen, the 8th King's Royal Irish Light Dragoons are now wearing blue coats decorated with white lace or corps and the collar, cuffs and turnbacks are scarlet. The change to blue, a general requisite regarding light dragoon regiments, had occurred in 1784. Original facings were permitted under the new regulation, but as the 8th was now a royal regiment their new blue coats were required to have scarlet. An interesting note that appeared in the regimental records mentions how as an economy measure around 1781, the men's jacket were made out of old cloaks.

The helmet being worn is the Tarleton which was made up of a leather skull with a peak in front, a turban round the base and a large black fur crest that reached across the top of the headdress from back to front. On the right side a metal plate bearing the badge of an Irish Harp and crown, and on the left a tall white-over-red feather plume. *(Image courtesy of the Anne SK Brown Military Collection, Brown University Library)*

3 – 8th Hussars, c1830 From 1830 all regular army regiments were required to exchange their white or silver lace for yellow or gold. At the same time William IV's love of the red coat saw the introduction of scarlet pelisses for hussars instead of blue. Richard Simkin's original watercolour of 1882 illustrates how the garment was worn slung over the left shoulder and how the many buttons were domed in shape. Of the required scarlet, the pelisses has an edging of black fur. A black shako is now worn which has yellow cord lines and a curbed chin chain. Simkin has provided us with a detailed example of how the carbine was held by metal hook from the shoulder-belt. *(Image courtesy of the Anne SK Brown Military Collection, Brown University Library)*

4 – 8th King's Own Royal Irish Light Dragoons Published by Rudolf Ackermann on 18 May 1852, this detailed colour plate shows an officer wearing a blue jacket, pelisse and trousers. Queen Victoria had restored the blue pelisse to hussar regiments. The busby had also replaced the shako seen in Image 3 above, its bag being scarlet, the tall white feather plume coming from a scarlet base. Richly decorated with Russia braid and gold gimp chain loops, the front of the jacket has buttons all the way down from the top to the waist. The pelisse is described as follows in Dress Regulations: 'Blue cloth, braided similarly to jacket, with gimp and Russia braid; collar and cuffs of fur and a narrow edging of the same fur entirely round the pelisse, with inlets to the sleeves and welts; the sleeve, side-seams, welts, and hips, ornamented with gold lace and braiding; crimson silk lining, rich dead gold plaited necklines, relieved with bright gold sliders and olivet ends.' The blue horse furniture is richly decorated with the regimental badge of a crowned Irish harp in gold, surrounded by wreaths of silver shamrocks. The scarlet sabretache also shows the royal cypher. Mounted on a grey horse, the image also shows a trumpeter. The artwork for the plate was provided by Henry Martens, the engraving by John Harris.

5 – 8th Hussars and Sepoy, 1857 Like most other cavalry regiments, the 8th Hussars spent many years in India where to suit the climate, a number of changes in dress had to be made. In this original tinted wash drawing by Harry Payne, a plain white cap is being worn which has a flap at the back to protect the wearer's neck from the sun. Harry Payne has shown the hussar with a Sepoy soldier walking alongside. *(Image Courtesy of the Anne SK Brown Military Collection, Brown University Library)*

6 – 8th (King's Royal Irish) Hussars A postcard produced around 1909 and based on an original photograph. Note how the carbine is now transported when not in use, via a long leather holster on the right side.

9TH (QUEEN'S ROYAL) LANCERS

TITLES
1715 – Owen Wynne's Regiment of Dragoons, then by the name of successive colonels
1751 – 9th Dragoons
1783 – 9th Light Dragoons
1816 – 9th Regiment of Light Dragoons (Lancers)
1830 – 9th or (Queen's Royal) Light Dragoons (Lancers)
1861 – 9th (Queen's Royal) Lancers

BATTLE HONOURS
'Peninsula', 'Punniar', 'Sobraon', 'Chillianwallah', 'Goojerat', 'Punjaub', 'Delhi 1857', 'Lucknow', 'Charaslah', 'Kabul 1879', 'Kandahar 1880', 'Afghanistan 1878-80', 'Modder River', 'Relief of Kimberley', 'Paardeberg', 'South Africa 1899-1902'

RECOMMENDED FURTHER READING
Historical Record of the Ninth, or The Queen's Royal Regiment of Light Dragoons Lancers by Richard Cannon and published in London by John W Parker in 1841. Contains one colour plate of uniform. With eleven coloured plates, *The Ninth (Queen's Royal) Lancers, 1715-1903* which was written by Frank H Reynard and published in 1904 by the Edinburgh firm of William Blackwood & Sons. In 1939, Gale & Polden published *The Ninth Queen's Royal Lancers, 1715-1936* by Major EW Sheppard, a 439-page work which includes ten uniform plates.

IMAGES

1 – 9th Dragoons, 1751 The regiment's first colonel, Owen Wynne, was succeeded in 1719 by James Crofts, by Richard Molesworth in 1732, Sir John Cope in 1737 and John Brown in 1742. Richard Simkin painted a private of the regiment at this time who he shows as wearing a long scarlet coat with buff tabs on the collar, buff cuffs, waistcoat, turnbacks and breeches. Dismounted and standing holding a musket, the soldier has a black hat edged with white lace, a white cord hanging from behind the right shoulder and a large buff belt holding a pouch. The buttons are arranged singularly down the front of the coat. Moving on to 1751 and an original watercolour painting by Reginald Augustus Wymer bearing that date, where we have a similar uniform being worn by a member of what is now the 9th Dragoons. The artist shows a mounted soldier who this time has his buttons arranged in pairs. There is a silver or white epaulette on the right shoulder and the embroidery on the buff horse furniture suggests a trophy of arms design. *(Image courtesy of the Anne SK Brown Military Collection, Brown University Library)*

2 – 9th Light Dragoons, 1815 Included in WY Carman's superb book, *Richard Simkin's Uniforms of the British Army The Cavalry Regiments,* is a full-page colour plate showing three members of the regiment. The first two figures are dated 1784 and show the blue jackets introduced that year. The facings are still buff, as are the turnbacks and shoulder belts. Dated 1812, the third figure, an officer, continues with the blue, but this time the coat has a scarlet collar and wide scarlet lapels. Reginald Augustus Wymer painted the same dress, this time with a date of 1815. As in the Simkin painting, gold epaulettes are on each shoulder, the pouch-belt is gold with a central scarlet stripe, and gold cord cap lines fall from the headdress down, passing under the right arm, across the chest until secured just below the left epaulette. The horse furniture and sabretache are dark blue with a wide gold edging and embroidered crowned GR cypher. *(Image courtesy of the Anne SK Brown Military Collection, Brown University Library)*

3 – 9th or (Queen's Royal) Light Dragoons (Lancers). 1850 Part of the Anne SK Brown Military Collection, this busy watercolour by Michael Angelo Hayes is dated 1850. There had been a short period from 1831 when red coats were worn by the regiment, but when the blue returned in 1840, May of that year saw a change in facing colour to scarlet. In the painting, much is going on. To the left the mounted band sit with their instruments, their plumes being red as opposed to the regimental black. There is a detailed rear view of the kettledrummer and the scarlet drum banner with its crossed lances and crown embroidery.

Moving now to the right side of the image, two officers are in conversation. One is wearing a stable dress jacket, blue, single-breasted with a scarlet collar three inches deep and edged with gold lace, gold cord shoulder straps and scarlet pointed cuffs. His cap is of blue cloth with a gold oak-leaf band, the top having a gold netted button with gold braid crossing. Featured, and holding the horse of one of the officers is a trooper, his right arm passing through a white leather strap which keeps his lance in place. The bottom of the weapon rests in a leather cup just by the foot. His mount, unlike that in his charge, has no throat

plume. Note how the shabraques, with their crossed lances insignia, do not carry the usual VR cypher, but instead have the reversed AR of Queen Adelaide. *(Image courtesy of the Anne SK Brown Military Collection, Brown University Library)*

4 – 9th (Queen's Royal) Lancers, c1899 Between 7 January 1888 and 6 September 1902, George Berridge & Co of 179 and 180 Upper Thames Street, London produced a series of chromoliths after Richard Simkin as supplements to the *Army and Navy Gazette*. Published on 6 July 1889, here we have Supplement No 19 which shows the blue coat now with the familiar lancer plastron in scarlet. The change to the tunic front, as seen in Image 3, had taken place just before 1880. The plume is now a mixture of black and white feathers, the cap plate according to Dress Regulations being '…in gilt or gilding metal the universal plate with the Royal Arms, on either side on sprays of laurel scrolls inscribed with the honours of the regiment. On a scroll below, Royal Lancers. In silver, on the centre of the plate, AR reversed and intertwined.'

5 – Kettledrummer and Drum Horse Taken from WJ Gordon's book *Bands of the British Army,* this illustration by Frederick Stansell possibly shows the cream coloured horse presented to the regiment in 1911 by King George V. Note how the kettledrummer's cap plume is scarlet instead of the regimental black and white. The scarlet drum banners are edged all round with gold lace, the embroider having crossed lances, the reversed AR cypher and numerous battle honours displayed on blue scrolls.

10TH (PRINCE OF WALES'S OWN ROYAL) HUSSARS

TITLES
1715 – Humphrey Gore's Regiment of Dragoons, then known by name of successive colonels
1751 – 10th Dragoons
1783 – 10th or Prince of Wales's Own Light Dragoons
1806 – 10th or Prince of Wales's Own Hussars
1811 – 10th (Prince of Wales's Own Royal) Hussars

BATTLE HONOURS
'Warburg', 'Peninsula', 'Waterloo', 'Sevastopol', 'Ali Masjid', 'Afghanistan 1878-79', 'Egypt 1884', 'Relief of Kimberley', 'Paardeberg', 'South Africa 1899-1902'

RECOMMENDED FURTHER READING
Historical Records of the Tenth, or The Prince of Wales's Own Royal Regiment of Hussars by Richard Cannon and published in London by John W Parker in 1843. Contains one colour plate of uniform. Also, by Colonel RS Liddell, *The Memoirs of the Tenth Royal Hussars (Prince of Wales's Own),* published by Longmans, Green & Co, London, 1891. Contains twelve colour plates of uniform.

Images

1 – 1715-83 Colonel RS Liddell's *The Memoirs of the Tenth Royal Hussars (Prince of Wales's Own)* was published in London by Longmans, Green & Co in 1891. It contains twelve colour plates signed 'O Norie', the litho work credited to W Greve of Berlin. Along with Richard Simkin and Harry Payne, Orlando Norie was possibly the most prolific British military artist of the nineteenth century. He was born in Bruges, Belgium on 15 January 1832 and, having settled in Dunkirk, went on to produce much of his work for the publishing and bookselling firm of Rudolf Ackermann. After his death in 1901, he was buried in Dunkirk's old cemetery close to that of the Commonwealth War Graves Commission.

The plate illustrated is the first to appear in the book and carries the date of 1715-83. As a regiment of Dragoons, the 10th had been raised in 1715 under the title of Gore's Regiment (Colonel Humphrey Gore) and, during the years taking it up to 1783, saw service in England and during the Scottish Rebellion of 1745. The 10th Dragoons later took part in operations in France and Germany during the Seven Years War and were present at the Battles of Minden, Warburg and Campen before returning home.

Orlando Norie's plate features two dragoons, one side on, the other with his back to the viewer, each wearing scarlet coats with yellow facings. Note the wide yellow turnbacks on the skirts and the deep cuffs and collars. Just seen are white breeches, the large black boots reaching far above the knee. The hats are black edged with silver lace. Also note the silver aiguillettes hanging from the right shoulder, these later to be discarded and replaced by epaulettes. On 1 July 1751, a Royal Warrant was issued dealing with the clothing of regiments. For the 10th, included in the directions was mention of buttonholes worked with white lace and that the breeches were now to be deep yellow. It would be in 1783 that following the change that year in style to Light Dragoons, the regiment in consequence altered its dress from scarlet to blue.

2 – 1783-1803 In 1783 an order was issued directing that the then 10th Dragoons should be formed into a regiment of light dragoons. At the same time the following was received from the Adjutant General, William Fawcett on 27 September: 'It is His Majesty's pleasure that the Tenth Regiment of Light Dragoons shall in future be called the Tenth or Prince of Wales's Own Regiment of Light Dragoons.' In consequence of becoming light dragoons, the necessary changes in equipment followed, including a change in dress to

blue. In the second of Orlando Norie's prints, which has been given the caption of 1783-1808, we see a clear rear view of a short blue jacket with yellow collar, cuffs and skirt turnbacks. Tarleton helmets are being worn with yellow and crimson turbans and tall yellow feather plumes. The waistcoats are blue, the lace and breeches white. Yellow also for the horse furniture which has silver lace lines edged with scarlet cloth. Holding his horse, an officer wears his blue cloak which is lined with yellow.

3 – Officer of the 10th (The Prince of Wales's Own) Royal Regiment of Hussars 'On the 18th May, 1831', records Colonel Liddell, 'a general order was issued ordering the colour of the hussar pelisses to be scarlet instead of blue, and the fur to be changed from white (authorized in 1823) to black.' This change is shown in a print after L Mansion and L Eschauzier. Featuring a mounted officer, the jacket is now all dark blue and greatly adorned with gold lace and cord.

4 – 10th Hussars, 1846-55 (India) Colonel RS Liddell recalls how early in March 1846 the regiment had received orders to prepare for service in the East Indies. At the time, the 10th Hussars were at home, parts of the regiment being found at York, Newcastle, Bradford and Leeds. Between 30 April and 7 May headquarters and the several troops arrived at Gravesend where they were embarked on board four transports, the *Brahmin*, *Larkin*, *Hindostan* and *Persia*. By 8 May the whole of the regiment was on its way to India. Orland Norie's painting for the period 1846-55 shows a camp scene, the men all wearing white tropical uniforms.

The Colonel notes how soon after arrival in India it was that the regiment's usual dress was found not to be suitable for the local climate. With this in mind the busby was replaced by a shako and 'with as little delay as possible after arrival at Kirkee the regiment was provided with white cotton clothing for ordinary wear.' The cloth used for the stable jackets and overalls seen in Orland Norie's image was a material known as American drill. A white cotton quilted cover was worn over the shako which had a curtain hanging down in such a position as to protect both the temples and back of the head. The 10th Hussars spent Christmas 1854 at Kirkee, leaving on 28 December for Bombay where transports were boarded for Egypt. The British having landed in the Crimea during the previous September, the regiment joining them there as reinforcements for the Cavalry Division during April 1855.

5 – The Badge and it's Wearer The dress of hussar regiments had undergone a number of changes during the Crimean War. Seen here in this postcard after Harry Payne, is the tunic as laid down in the 1861 edition of *Regulations for the Dress of General, Staff, and Regimental Officers of The Army*: 'tunic, entirely of blue cloth; single-breasted; the collar two inches high, rounded in front. On each side of the breast, six loops of gold chain lace, with caps and drops, fastening with six gold worked olivets; the top loop eight inches long, the bottom one four inches.' Here also is the fur busby which has a scarlet bag and white plume. The artist has placed the cap badge in the top left-hand corner of the image.

11th Prince Albert's Own Hussars

TITLES
1715 - Philip Honywood's Regiment of Dragoons, then by the name of successive colonels
1751 – 11th Dragoons
1783 – 11th Light Dragoons
1840 – 11th Prince Albert's Own Regiment of Hussars

BATTLE HONOURS
The Sphinx superscribed 'Egypt', 'Warburg', 'Beaumont', 'Willems', 'Salamanca', 'Peninsula', 'Waterloo', 'Bhurtpore', 'Alma', 'Balaclava', 'Inkerman', Sevastopol'

RECOMMENDED FURTHER READING
Historical Record of the Eleventh, or The Prince Albert's Own Regiment of Hussars by Richard Cannon and published by John W Parker, London, 1843. Contains one coloured plate of uniform. Also by Captain Trevelyan Williams, *The Historical Records of the Eleventh Hussars Prince Albert's Own*. Published by George Newnes, London, 1908 and with twelve colour plates of uniform.

IMAGES
1 – 11th Dragoons, 1760 The *Clothing* book of 1742 shows that the coats of what was then Lord Mark Kerr's Regiment of Dragoons (commissioned 29 May 1732) were red with buff cuffs and linings. The waistcoats were also buff, and the breeches red. Richard Simkin painted a mounted figure of this period wearing a black hat trimmed with white and wearing a wide buff belt holding a large pouch on the right side. The horse furniture is also buff and decorated with a trophy of arms. A second painting by the same artist is dated 1751 and this shows

the coat with white-laced buttonholes and cuffs similarly decorated. The buff waistcoat is edged all round with white lace, as are its two pocket flaps. The breeches are now buff, and the figure wears a crimson sash over the right shoulder which terminates in a knot on the left side.

The original watercolour illustrated is by Reginald Augustus Wymer. Dated 1760, the artist shows buff patches of the collar, a buff waistcoat and buff turnbacks. The same buff pouch-belt is worn and Wymer shows this passing under the scarlet strap on the left shoulder. The buttons are arranged in groups of three. The horse furniture lost its trophy of arms and is now plain, save for XI above the letter D on a red ground within a wreath. The edging is white and green. For the holster cap, the royal cypher and at the bottom edge, XI D in white. The same dress was depicted by David Morier in a painting belonging to the Royal Collection at Windsor, nine years earlier. *(Image courtesy of the Anne SK Brown Military Collection, Brown University Library)*

2 – 11th Dragoons, c1760 After PW Reynolds, this colour plate from Captain Trevelyan Williams's regimental history, shows a clear view of the uniform mentioned above from a different angle. See the white cord aiguillette attached to the shoulder and how the coat tails were pleated. At the back of the saddle, a rolled red cloak showing a buff lining. The black leather cap has a metal crest and a white-over-red plume. At the front, a cloth flap embroidered with the royal cypher.

3 – Officer of the 11th Light Dragoons, 1812 In this original watercolour painting by J Howson we see an officer of the now 11th Light Dragoons wearing the broad-topped shako introduced in 1812. The lace around the top is silver and the white-over-red short plume rises from a gold boss. Note how the gold cap lines cross the front of the headdress and having been attached to the top then fall down to a fixture on the chest lace. Blue coats with silver lace had been assumed in 1784. A narrow pouch-belt is being worn with silver pickers, and a crimson sash around the waist. *(Image courtesy of the Anne SK Brown Military Collection, Brown University Library)*

4 – An 11th Light Dragoon – In this gruesome image published by D Ash of 27 Fetter Lane, London on 26 April 1826, we see a member of the regiment having just parted the head of an enemy cavalryman with his sword. This hand-coloured engraving was part of a set fourteen produced by D Ash between 1 February 1826 to 6 January 1827, the majority, if not

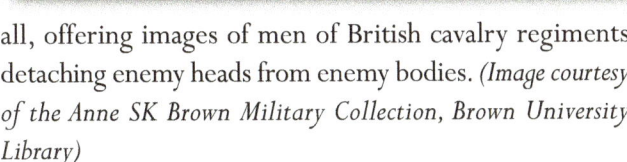

all, offering images of men of British cavalry regiments detaching enemy heads from enemy bodies. *(Image courtesy of the Anne SK Brown Military Collection, Brown University Library)*

5 – Prince Albert's Own, or The Royal Eleventh Hussar The uniform detail, and even the titles given to the engravings forming the set mentioned in Image 4 above, can not always be relied upon for accuracy. The images certainly do, however, form welcome additions to any collection of military prints. The same must be said of sheet music covers of which during Victorian times many were produced featuring uniformed subjects. Illustrated, and from the Anne SK Brown Military Collection, is a delightful example of the uniform worn by the 11th Prince Albert's Own Regiment of Hussars about 1845, but it must be mentioned that the word 'Royal' formed no part of the title at this time. But all seems well with the uniform, the artist correctly making the jacket and pelisse red as directed by William IV in 1830. *(Image courtesy of the Anne SK Brown Military Collection, Brown University Library)*

6th – 11th Hussars, Postcard Accuracy is almost guaranteed when it comes to the work of artist Harry Payne. When creating the artwork for this Raphael Tuck & Sons, Ltd postcard, the artist would have been well aware of those essential tools for any military artist, Dress Regulations for Officers of the Army. For the black sable fur busby, 'A gold gimp oval cockade, 2 inches deep and 1½ inches wide, in the centre in front, the top on a level with the top of the busby.' There would be a spring socket behind the cockade which held the plume of an ostrich feather, '…15 inches high from the top of the busby to the top of the plume; encircled by a ring. Vulture feather bottom in a corded gilt ball socket with four upright leaves.'

The blue cloth tunic is edged all round with gold chain gimp, the top of the collar having ¾-inch gold lace. On each side of the breast there are six loops of gold chain gimp, with caps and drops fastened with gold-worked olivets. Gold Austrian knots decorate the bottom of each sleeve. The pantaloons, crimson cloth, a distinctive colour for the 11th Hussars which led to their nickname, 'The Cherubims'. You may, however, prefer the name thought up by the scriptwriters of the film 'The Charge of The Light Brigade' who had Lord Cardigan referring to his regiment as 'my Cherry Bums'.

12th (Prince of Wales's Royal) Lancers

Titles
1715 – Phineas Bowles's Dragoons, changing later to names of successive colonels
1751 – 12th Dragoons
1768 – 12th (Prince of Wales's) Light Dragoons
1816 – 12th (Prince of Wales's) Lancers
1817 – 12th (Prince of Wales's Royal) Lancers

Battle Honours
The Sphinx superscribed 'Egypt', 'Peninsula', 'Waterloo', 'South Africa 1851-2-3', 'Sevastopol', 'Central India', 'Relief of Kimberley', 'Paardeberg', 'South Africa 1899-1902'

Recommended Further Reading
Historical Record of the Twelfth, or The Prince of Wales's Own Royal Regiment of Lancers by Richard Cannon and published by John W Parker, London, 1842. Contains one coloured plate of uniform. Also *The History of the XII Royal Lancers (Prince of Wales's)* by Captain PT Stewart which was published by the Oxford University Press in 1950.

Images
1 – Colonel Alexander Rose's Regiment of Dragoons Major-General Phineas Bowles was succeeded by his son, also named Phineas, as colonel of the regiment in March 1719. He was followed by Alexander Rose at the end of 1740 and illustrated is Richard Simkin's account of the uniform worn about that time. The private wears a red coat which has a white worsted shoulder-knot on the right side, white patches of the collar, white cuffs and turnbacks. The breeches are red, the wide shoulder-belt, pouch and gauntlet gloves, buff. Just visible in the painting is the pocket flap of a white waistcoat.

Moving on now to 1751, uniform authority WY Carman records that in that year a supply of scarlet and white cloth, together with 359 dozen silver buttons, was received in Ireland where the regiment was then stationed.

The David Morier painting of that year held in the Royal Collection at Windsor

shows a mounted private of the now 12th Dragoons wearing much the same dress as shown by Simkin, but the breeches are now white. The shabraque and holster caps are white with a green stripe running through white lace.

2 – 12th (Prince of Wales's) Light Dragoons, c1768 Along with the new title in 1768 came a change of facing colour from white to black. The coat now had black lapels with white buttons, the headdress a black helmet with the peak turned up at the front, the top having a metal comb from which flowed short black hair. A red turban was worn around the base. As can be seen in this original watercolour painting by E Fitzgerald, the waistcoats and breeches were white. The artist also shows a pattern of horse furniture which is thought to have been unique to the 12th Light Dragoons: black with strips of white goatskin. Now with the Prince of Wales connection, the regiment was permitted to display his plumes, coronet and motto insignia, along with the devices of a rising sun and red dragon. With smaller figures fighting in the background, the artist has depicted his 12th Light Dragoon in an action scene. With his sword raised high ready to strike, a Prussian hussar wearing a black uniform takes careful aim with his carbine. *(Image courtesy of the Anne SK Brown Military Collection, Brown University Library)*

3 – 12th Lancers, 1742 to 1842 The third illustration is an example of one of the many watercolour paintings by Richard Simkin that featured several figures wearing uniforms worn by the regiment at different times during its history. At top left and dated 1742, a mounted figure of Colonel Phineas Bowles's Dragoons, his red coat and breeches, white facings and buff equipment much the same as seen in Image 1, but we can now seen the trophy of arms decoration on the horse furniture. Along to the right the next figure is dated 1794 and the jacket is now blue with a yellow collar and cuffs, this change having occurred ten years earlier.

Moving to the centre of the painting we have a group dated 1814, led by an officer wearing a wide-topped shako with a white-over-red plume, silver lace and ornaments. The jacket, with its wide plastron-style lapels, provides a clear view of the regiment's yellow, the same colour appearing on the collar and pointed cuffs. With sword drawn, its empty steel scabbard can be seen behind a blue-faced sabretache which has silver lace all round and carries a crowned GR cypher.

In 1831 scarlet jackets replaced the blue. Providing an interesting side-on view to the bottom left figure Richard Simkin shows the elaborate pouch-belt, described in Dress Regulations as being of 'gold lace, two inches wide, with half-inch silk stripe, morocco lining and edging to correspond with waist-belt; silver plate with pickers and chains. Buckle, tip, and slide.' The pouch-box was of scarlet leather with gold embroidered edging round the top, a solid silver flap ornamented with gilt royal cypher. The richly decorated blue sabretache and shabraque are embroidered with the reversed and intertwined WR cypher with crown above, the lower sections having crossed lances with red-over-white pennants, the Prince of Wales's plumes, coronet and motto in silver and gold, the numeral XII and a Sphinx superscribed 'Egypt'. Both are trimmed with two-inch

PLAYER'S CIGARETTES.
5

12TH LANCERS;
Officer's full dress cap, 1859-81.

gold lace. For the last figure (bottom right) we have the all blue uniform, with its red facings, adopted in 1842. *(Image courtesy of the Anne SK Brown Military Collection, Brown University Library)*

4 – 'Jolly Songs' Lancers Charles Godfrey (1866-1935) was a bandmaster with the Royal Horse Guards and he is credited as the arranger in 1883 for 'Jolly Songs', published by Howard & Co of 25 Great Marlborough Street, London. The sheet music cover chosen shows a mounted officer of what appears to be the 12th Lancers. Certainly, the red plastron, cap top and plume suggest this and also, of course, the 12 over L below the crossed lances on the shabraque. But there seems to be a suggestion of a 17th Lancers-type skull and crossbones device too. Sheet music covers will always represent delightful additions to military print collections, albeit that their accuracy cannot always be relied upon. HC Maguire was responsible for the artwork, CB Court of 46 Portland Street, London for the litho work.

5 – Officer's Full Dress Cap, 1859-81 From the set of cigarette cards featuring military headdress published by John Player & Son in 1931 a detailed study of an officer's cap. *(Image courtesy of the Anne SK Brown Military Collection, Brown University Library)*

13th Hussars

Titles
1715 – Richard Munden's Regiment of Dragoons, then by name of successive colonels
1751 – 13th Dragoons
1783 – 13th Light Dragoons
1861 – 13th Hussars

Battle Honours
'Albuhera', 'Vittoria', 'Orthes', 'Toulouse', 'Peninsula', 'Waterloo', 'Alma', 'Balaclava', 'Inkerman', 'Sevastopol', 'Relief of Ladysmith', 'South Africa 1899-1902'

Recommended Further Reading
Historical Record of the Thirteenth Regiment of Light Dragoons by Richard Cannon and published by John W Parker, London, 1842. Contains one colour plate of uniform. Also *History of The XIII Hussars* by CRB Barrett published by William Blackwood & Sons, Edinburgh, 1911. A two-volume work which has six colour plates of uniform.

Images
1 – Humphrey Bland's Regiment of Dragoons, 1742 Richard Munden was succeeded by Sir Robert Rich in November 1722, by the 1st Earl of Harrington, William Stanhope in September 1725, Henry Hawley, July 1730, Robert Dalway, May 1740, then at the beginning of 1741, Humphrey Bland. In this original watercolour by Reginald Augustus Wymer, the artist shows, wearing a scarlet coat with green facings, a private of Colonel Humphrey Bland's Dragoons. The waistcoat and breeches are white and the equipment, buff leather. *(Image courtesy of the Anne SK Brown Military Collection, Brown University Library)*

2 – 13th Dragoons, Officer c1751 The regiment now known as 13th Dragoons rather than their colonel's name,

Richard Simkin's painting shows the green facings more clearly than the Wymer image above. The collar has green patches with a single gold laced buttonhole, the cuffs are green, which are just visible above the buff gauntlet glove. One change, green now for the breeches and coat turnbacks. For the buff waistcoat, the officer has gold lace edging down the front and along the bottom; the same for the pocket flap.

3 – 13th Light Dragoons, Officer c1810 Blue had replaced the scarlet in 1784, the facing at the same time changing to buff. In this second watercolour by Reginald Augustus Wymer from the Anne SK Brown Military Collection, the officer is seen in a short jacket decorated across the chest, down the front and along the bottom edge, in double lines on the collar, and on the sleeves with gold cord. He wears a red leather pouch-belt with gold lace and a similar, but narrower, belt for the sword. The headdress is the Tarleton helmet, with a white-over-red plume issuing from a gilt holder, and his black leather boots have gold edgings and tassels at the top. *(Image courtesy of the Anne SK Brown Military Collection, Brown University Library)*

4 – 13th Hussars Painted by Orlando Norie, this watercolour shows the regiment out in open country on exercise. The uniforms are blue with white facings, the tunics having gold or yellow cord across the chest. The fur busby has a white plume, the gold cords of which hang from the rear of the headdress then cross around the neck to end in olivets. *(Image courtesy of the Anne SK Brown Military Collection, Brown University)*

5 – Kettledrummer, c1898 Mr RG Harris produced an extremely comprehensive series of articles for the Military Historical Society on mounted bands, their drum horses and banners during the 1960s. In November 1967 (*The Bulletin,* Volume XVIII, No 70) the 13th Hussars were featured, the author in this article telling how the regiment had returned to England from overseas service in November 1885 where it remained enjoying a comparatively long period at home before going to South Africa and the Boer War.

An Army Order No 38 issued on 1 February 1890 authorised the 13th Hussars to include among their appointments the additional battle honours of 'Alma', 'Vittoria', 'Orthes' and 'Toulouse'. With this, notes RG Harris, 'It is almost certain that new banners were procured about this time….' We can see these here in one of the chromolith colour plates after Frederick Stansell that were used to illustrate *Bands of the British Army* by WJ Gordon, published by Frederick Warne & Co, London, about 1914. Of the regimental white facing colour, the banners display the new battle honours along with those previously authorised on blue scrolls.

Frederick Stansell seems to have based his painting on a large skewbald drum horse named 'General' and his rider for many years, Corporal Oliver who had handed his drumsticks over to another drummer by June 1898. A photograph included with Mr Harris's article dated 1903-4, shows a black horse and a shabraque which he describes as '…blue edged with silver and an ER cypher with crown above on the hind corners.'

6 – Colonel Robert Baden-Powell, The Hero of Mafeking A coloured print after a photograph, the founder of the Boy Scout Movement is seen here in the uniform of a field officer of the 13th Hussars. Robert Baden-Powell had joined the regiment with the rank of lieutenant in 1876 and after service in South Africa was given command of the 5th Dragoon Guards in India. Returning to Africa he would play an important role during the Siege of Mafeking and it was here that he would acquire is 'Hero Of Mafeking' nickname. The siege over on 16 May 1900, Baden-Powell, now a national hero, was then promoted to major-general.

For a description of the uniform worn in the photograph we read from the 1900 edition of Dress Regulations the following: 'Tunic—Blue cloth, edged all round with gold chin gimp. The collar edged along the top with ¾-inch lace. On each side of the breast six loops of gold chain gimp, with caps and drops fastening with gold-worked olivets. On each back-seam a double line of the same gimp, forming three eyes at the top, passing under a netted cap at the waist, and ending in an Austrian knot reaching to the bottom of the skirt, with a tracing of gold braid all round the gimp. An Austrian knot of gold chain gimp on each sleeve, reaching to 8 inches from the bottom of the cuff.' As field officer, the braiding on the sleeve surrounding the Austrian knot extends eleven inches from the bottom of the cuff.

The black sable fur busby has a gold gimp oval cockade which has a spring socket behind to hold the fifteen-inch ostrich feather plume. Falling down the right side, a busby bag of white cloth with gold braid lines terminating with a gold gimp button.

14th (King's) Hussars

TITLES
1715 – James Dormer's Regiment of Dragoons, afterwards by the name of successive colonels
1751 – 14th Dragoons
1776 – 14th Light Dragoons
1798 – 14th or Duchess of York's Own Light Dragoons
1830 – 14th King's Light Dragoons
1861 – 14th (King's) Hussars

BATTLE HONOURS
'Douro', 'Talavera', 'Fuentes d' Onor', Salamanca', 'Vittoria', 'Pyrenees', 'Orthes', 'Peninsula', 'Chillianwallah', 'Goojerat', 'Punjab', 'Persia', 'Central India', 'Relief of Ladysmith', 'South Africa 1900-02'

RECOMMENDED FURTHER READING
Historical Record of the Fourteenth, or the King's Regiment of Light Dragoons by Richard Cannon and published by Parker, Furnivall & Parker, London, 1847. Includes one colour plate of uniform. Also *Historical Record of the 14th (King's) Hussars From 1715 to AD 1900* which was written by Colonel Henry Blackburne Hamilton and published by Longmans, Green & Co, London, 1901. Includes twelve colour plates of uniform.

IMAGES
1 – 15th Light Dragoons, c1776 Brigadier-General James Dormer's regiment are on record as having worn scarlet, the 1742 *Clothing* book providing greater detail for what was then Archibald Hamilton's Regiment of Dragoons. Showing a mounted private, the image shows a red coat faced with light yellow collar patches, linings, waistcoat and breeches. The horse furniture being of the same colour embroidered with a trophy of arms. The David Morier painting of the regiment held in the Royal Collection at Windsor dated 1751 illustrated much the same uniform, the horse furniture however now yellow, its white lace having one red and one green stripe, and bearing the royal cypher. The holster caps carry the numerical designation XIV D in red.

For the same year Richard Cannon includes the following a lengthy description of uniform and horse furniture:

Coats – scarlet; double-breasted, without lapels, lined with lemon colour; slit sleeves turned up with lemon colour; the button-holes worked with narrow white lace; the buttons of white metal, set on three and three; a long slash pocket in each skirt; and a white worsted aiguillette on the right shoulder.

Waistcoats and Breeches – lemon colour.

Hats – Bound with silver lace, and ornamented with a white loop and a black cockade. Red forage cap turned up with lemon colour, and XIV. D. on the flap.

Boots – Of jacked leather reaching the knee.

Cloaks – Scarlet, with a lemon-coloured cape; the buttons set on three on three, upon white frogs or loops, with a red and green stripe down the centre.

Horse Furniture – Of lemon-coloured cloth; the holster caps and housings having a border of white lace, with red and green stripe down the centre; XIV.D. embroidered upon a red ground, within a wreath of roses and thistles, on the housing; and upon the holster caps G.R., with the crown over it, and XIV.D. underneath.

Officers – Distinguished by silver lace and embroidery; and a crimson silk sash worn across the left shoulder.

Quarter Masters – To wear a crimson sash round their waists.

Sergeants – To have narrow silver lace on the cuffs, pockets, and shoulder-straps; silver aiguillettes; and green, red, and white worsted sashes tied round their waists.

Drummers and Hautboys – Clothed in lemon coloured coats, lined and faced with scarlet, and ornamented with white lace, having a red and green stripe down the centre: red waistcoats and breeches.

Illustrated is a light dragoon of around 1776, one of the colour plates after Richard Simkin that were included in *Historical Record of the 14th (King's) Hussars From 1715 to AD 1900* by Colonel Henry Blackburne Hamilton. The regiment's lemon yellow is much in evidence on the collar, cuffs and lapels, the latter reaching down to the waist. White or silver epaulettes are worn on each shoulder, the lace also being of silver or white. White cloth has been used for the waistcoat and the headdress has a yellow and red turban, a flowing red plume rising out of a gilt metal crest and the GR cypher on a flap at the front. As before, the horse furniture is yellow with lines of green and red on white lace.

2 – Officer (Lieut Col) of the 14th Light Dragoons In Parade Dress Published in April 1812, this colour plate drawn by Charles Hamilton Smith and aquatinted by LC Stadler shows the regiment now with orange facings. The regiment had taken the name of the Duchess of York in 1798, who as the Princess Royal of Prussia they had escorted upon her arrival in England to marry the Duke. In the following year they had been given permission to adopt the Prussian eagle as its badge, along with orange facings, this being the livery colour of the House of Brandenburg.

The uniform is that ordered for light dragoon regiments in 1811. The jacket has short tails, the facing colour being used for the collar, pointed cuffs, lapels, turnbacks and piping. Regarding the wide lapels with their ten buttons on each, the image shows them fastened back, but in marching order they were buttoned across revealing only the blue side. Silver epaulettes with bullion fringes and badges of rank are worn on each shoulder. The shako has a silver lace upper band, a silver cockade and a white-over-red plume.

3 – Officers and Trooper, 1836 As well as Richard Simkin, J Mathews and William Griggs both supplied artwork for Colonel Henry Blackburne Hamilton's 1901 regimental history. Image 2 is after the latter and features two mounted officers and a private all in scarlet jackets. The change from blue had occurred just before 1830, the year that William IV had granted the regiment the title of 14th (King's) Light Dragoons. Now a royal regiment, the facings could now be exchanged for the blue seen in the illustration.

4 – 14th Light Dragoons, c1836 – Painted in 1882 by Richard Simkin, this original watercolour shows a clear rear view of the uniform worn by troopers. Note

how the yellow cap lines are attached to the side of the shako then fall to be taken around to the front. White metal shoulder scales are being worn, both the blue collar and cuffs having yellow braid edgings. Clearly visible is the metal hook on the white leather shoulder-belt used to secure the carbine. *(Image courtesy of the Anne SK Brown Military Collection, Brown University Library)*

5 – 14th (King's) Hussars Clearly seen in this original 1909 artwork by Ernest Ibbetson is the regiment's Prussian eagle badge, seen here on the collar and on a yellow cloth ground above the chevrons. Note how the old lemon yellow regimental colour is now being used for the busby bag. *(Image courtesy of the Anne SK Brown Military Collection, Brown University Library)*

15TH (THE KING'S) HUSSARS

TITLES
1759 – 15th Light Dragoons
1766 – 1st or The King's Light Dragoons
1769 – 15th or The King's Light Dragoons
1807 – 15th (or the King's) Light Dragoons (Hussars)
1861 – 15th (The King's) Hussars

BATTLE HONOURS
'Merebimur', 'Emsdorff', 'Villers-en-Cauchies', 'Willems', 'Egmont-op-Zee', 'Sahagun', 'Vittoria', 'Peninsula', 'Waterloo', Afghanistan 1878-80'

RECOMMENDED FURTHER READING
Historical Record of the Fifteenth, or, The King's Regiment of Light Dragoons, Hussars by Richard Cannon and published by

John W Parker, London, 1841. Contains one colour plate of uniform. Also, and with twelve colour plates of uniform, *XVth (The King's) Hussars, 1759 to 1913* which was written by Colonel HC Wylly and published by Caxton Publishing Company, Ltd, London, 1914.

IMAGES

1 – A Light Dragoon of the 15th Regiment, Commonly Called Major General Elliot's Light Horse – George Augustus Eliott (his surname seems to have gained an 'L' but lost a 'T' in the caption) was held in high esteem by King George II who had placed him at the head of the light cavalry during the expeditions against the French coast in 1758. It followed that in March of the following year the monarch would choose Eliott to raise, form and discipline a new regiment—the 15th Light Dragoons. Regarding its creation, Cannon records: 'The formation of this Regiment was looked upon as an era in the military annals of the kingdom; and it was an event which created great public interest.' Acton, Knightsbridge and other places in the vicinity of London would provide rendezvous locations of the several troops raised.

Quickly the ranks of the regiment were filled: '…many respectable young men evinced great readiness to enrol themselves under its standards' (Cannon again) 'and a remarkable circumstance favoured its formation, as a number of journeymen tailors, and of clothiers, who had come to London to petition Parliament for relief from certain grievances, under which they considered themselves to labour, became ambitious of appearing in the uniform of this popular corps….'

In the engraving illustrated, published by T Jefferys of Charing Cross, London on 1 September 1760, a short scarlet coat with green collar and cuffs is being worn. The turnbacks are white, as are the laced button holes, waistcoat and breeches. Yellow or gold epaulettes are worn, the sword and pouch-belts being of white leather. The horse furniture appears blue with two yellow or gold lines, the holster cap having a crown above the royal cypher. The headdress takes the form of a copper cap enamelled black, with a brass crest from which flows red hair. Unclear in the image is the king's cypher and crown which was painted on the turned up flap at the front, together with the letters 'L' and 'D'. A clear view of this headdress being worn by a drummer can be seen on page 39 of Michael Barthorp's superb book, *British Cavalry Uniforms Since 1660*. *(Image courtesy of the Anne SK Brown Military Collection, Brown University Library)*

2 – An Officer of the 15th or King's Hussars, c1804 Blue coats were ordered to replace the red in 1784, the former colour now appearing as the regiment's facings. Image 2 is from the Anne SK Brown Military Collection who catalogue the picture as an original unsigned watercolour probably after Dennis Dighton. An interesting hand-written caption accompanies the image which notes how the work had been 'taken from life', the subject being one 'Major Forrester', the location 'Ipswich Barracks'.

Described as a 'tapering, felt truncated cone' the tall headdress being worn has a white-over-red plume, a length of gold cord encircling the cap before it falls to the back, and a long red bag on the right side. The jacket has bars of braid covering the front, gold also decorating the sides and pointed cuffs. Note how the grey overalls are held

in place by straps passing under the boots. The leather ends at the bottom are called bootings and were added to cavalry overalls around 1800. Major Francis Forester was noted by Cannon as being one of the officers that embarked at Portsmouth for the war in Spain in 1808. *(Image courtesy of the Anne SK Military Collection, Brown University Library)*

3 – Officer in Full Dress, 1807 Also from the Anne SK Brown Military Collection comes this magnificent study signed and dated by Robert Dighton and featuring a dismounted officer standing by his horse. Here again is the tall tapering felt cap with its tall white-over-red feather plume and red bag as seen in Image 2. Clearer now is the silver lace decoration of the collar and how it has been enclosed within a gold line of narrow lace. In full dress now, the grey overalls have been exchanged for white breeches. Dighton includes great detail in his painting; note how the snake-hook fastening and lion bosses of the narrow gold sword-belt are quite distinguishable. The horse furniture too, the interpretation of the silver embroidery on the holster cap doing much to identify the regiment's Emsdorff battle honour. *(Image courtesy of the Anne SK Military Collection, Brown University Library)*

4 – A Private of the XVth or King's Lt. Dns. (Hussars) Published in September 1812, this image after the work of Charles Hamilton Smith shows the Hungarian-style blue shabraque with its red 'wolf's-teeth' edging and embroidery. The cap is of brown fur, out of which comes a red bag and a white-over-red plume. The jacket has a red collar and cuffs, both of which are decorated with white cord, and rows of the same spread across the chest. The blue pelisse has an edging of black fur. The private, seen here priming his carbine, sits upon a white sheepskin which is edged with red braid.

5 – 15th (The King's) Hussars As military postcard authority Geoff White pointed out in his book, *Collecting British Army Postcards,* the History and Traditions series was probably the best known of all Gale & Polden military postcard sets. The company proudly advertise their product as being the only army postcards authorized by the War Office. The artwork supplied was by J McNeill in 1908, then Ernest Ibbetson from the following year. Divided roughly in half, each card showed a brief account of the regiment's history, along with a representation of its badge and battle honours. The artwork, Ernest Ibbetson's in this case, appeared on the left.

16TH (THE QUEEN'S) LANCERS

TITLES
1759 – 16th Light Dragoons
1766 – 2nd Queen's Light Dragoons
1769 – 16th or the Queen's Light Dragoons
1815 – 16th (The Queen's) Light Dragoons (Lancers)
1861 – 16th (The Queen's) Lancers

BATTLE HONOURS
'Beaumont', 'Willems', 'Talavera', 'Fuentes d' Onor', 'Salamanca', 'Vittoria', 'Nive', 'Peninsula', 'Waterloo', 'Rhurtpore', 'Ghuznee 1839', 'Affghanistan, 1839', 'Maharajpore', 'Aliwal', 'Sobraon', 'Relief of Kimberley', 'Paardeberg', 'South Africa 1900-02'

RECOMMENDED FURTHER READING
Richard Cannon, *Historical Record of the Sixteenth, or The Queen's Regiment of Light Dragoons, Lancers,* published in London by John W Parker in 1842. Contains one colour plate of uniform and covers the history from formation in 1759 until 1841. Taking the records from formation up to 1912 is *History of the Sixteenth, The Queen's Light Dragoons (Lancers)* by Colonel Henry Graham and published in 1912 by George Simpson. Includes eight colour plates of uniform.

IMAGES
1 – The Soldier's Daughter General John Burgoyne, playwright and politician, had raised the regiment and at first dressed it in red coats with black facings and white turnbacks. The waistcoats and breeches were also white. Blue collars and cuffs replaced the black when Queen's was introduced to the title in 1766. It was while fighting in America that Cornet Francis Geary, the eldest son of Admiral Francis Geary, was killed during an ambush near Flemington, New Jersey on 14 December 1776. His memorial in the south aisle of St Nicolas's Church, Great Bookham, Surrey, shows the young officer in uniform, a detailed example of his light dragoon crested helmet being included.

In 1784 the coats of light dragoon regiments were changed from red to blue. Illustrated is a song sheet entitled 'The Soldier's Daughter', the music of which was published by Henry Thompson of No 75 St Paul's Church Yard, London on 7 March 1803, which includes a soldier of the 16th Light Dragoons offering comforting arms to a young girl. Let the words tell the tale. The artwork for this image is credited to both Thomas Georg Ingall and Laurie & Whittle.

His white wig tied at the back with black ribbon is clearly visible below a Tarleton light cavalry helmet with black crest and red-over-white feather. The soldier's collar and cuffs are red, and gold or yellow lace decorates his coat, front and back. *(Image courtesy of the Anne SK Brown Military Collection, Brown University Library)*

2 – Charge of the 16th Lancers at the Battle of Aliwal On 28 January 1846 Sikh troops occupied a position four miles long between the villages of Aliwal and Bhundri in northern India. It was the time of the First Anglo-Sikh War and British forces of the East India Company led by General Sir Harry Smith had successfully captured Aliwal. An enemy counter attack soon followed in which a large body of Sikh infantry stood firm in a square formation ready to receive the oncoming charge of the 16th Lancers. Here we see the scene as set out by artist Henry Martens in the form of a print published by Rudolph Ackermann, Jnr from a engraving by John Harris.

In their scarlet jackets and blue overalls, on came the cavalrymen with their lances held ready. To the left one man can be seen about to thrust his deep into a fallen enemy, while a lancer further on riding a grey horse is about to lance another. All around lie dead and wounded blue-coated artillerymen, one of their guns now laying silent. As their mounted leader, seen on the extreme right of the image, urges his men on, the infantry of the Fauj-i-Ain in their white turbans seemed doomed.

A complete British success, General Smith later wrote: 'I have gained one of the most glorious battles ever fought in India …. Never was victory more complete, and never was one fought under more happy circumstances, literally with the pomp of a field day; and right well did all behave.' It had, however, cost the 16th Lancers 144 men out of some 300.

Regarding the uniform, by 1830 blue jackets had given way to scarlet and the plumes were now black cocktail feathers for officers, and black hair for the men. These would have been removed for active service. The trousers had changed to blue with double red stripes down each leg.

3 – Going to the Review Frederick Stansell, in his book *Our Armies,* has used both full and khaki service dress in this image which he captions 'Going To The Review, 16th Queen's Lancers.' The 16th held several distinctions. In 1846 at the battle of Aliwal during the First Sikh War, it was the first regiment British cavalry regiment to use the lance. And they were the only lancer regiment to wear

scarlet, this leading to the nickname 'The Scarlet Lancers.' The old scarlet cavalry coatee had disappeared during Crimean War, giving way to the now familiar lancer tunic with its wide plastron. The former double red trouser stripes were replaced in 1855 for the pale yellow seen in Frederick Stansell's painting.

The year of Stansell's publication (1902) and seeing the officer on the right in service dress, brings to mind that the beginning of the Great War was not far off. In its first weeks the 16th Lancers left Ireland for France and were soon in action at Mons. Amongst the cavalry, the sabre against lance argument had gone on for many years, but lancers retailed their lances and it would be in 1914 that the 16th proved the worth of the weapon as a charge led by Lieutenant Charles Tempest into a group of Jagers sent the enemy running from the field of battle. But soon modern warfare would prove the mounted soldier's role in battle redundant. As ever, the artist has included much detail in his painting. The officer in service dress has been given both Second Boer War campaign medals, and clear is the method by which the lances were carried via a white leather strap around the arm. This was to leave both hands free, if required, for guiding the horse.

17TH (DUKE OF CAMBRIDGE'S OWN) LANCERS

TITLES
1759 – 18th Light Dragoons
1763 – 17th Light Dragoons
1822 – 17th Light Dragoons (Lancers)
1876 – 17th (Duke of Cambridge's Own) Lancers

BATTLE HONOURS
'Alma', 'Balaclava', 'Inkerman', 'Sevastopol', 'Central India', 'South Africa 1879', 'South Africa 1900-02'.

RECOMMENDED FURTHER READING
Richard Cannon, *Historical Record of the Seventeenth Regiment of Light Dragoons: Lancers.* London, John W Parker, 1841. Covers the formation of the regiment in 1759 and of its subsequent records until 1841. Contains seven colour plates of uniform, Hon JW Fortescue, *A History of the 17th Lancers (Duke of Cambridge's Own).* London, Macmillan & Co, 1895. Contains thirteen colour plates of uniform.

DH Parry, *The Death or Glory Boys.* London, Cassell & Co Ltd, 1899.

IMAGES
1 – The 17th Light Dragoons On Service in America 1775 - Lieutenant-Colonel John Hale of the 47th Regiment of Foot, who had brought to England the despatches announcing the capture of Quebec and with it the

news of the death of General James Wolfe, raised a regiment styled as the 18th Light Dragoons under a warrant dated 7 November 1759. Recruiting took place around Watford and Rickmansworth, the colonel's family home being in Hertfordshire. Regarding uniform, Henry Manners Chichester and George Burges-Short noted in their book, *The Records and Badges of Every Regiment and Corps in the British Army*, that Colonel Hale chose the scarlet with white facings of his 47th Regiment, but the lace was of a white and black mixture. The same authors also make mention of the 'Morning paper' lace and how a 'Death or

Glory' badge was embroidered on the left breast of the coat to commemorate the fall of Wolfe. This, of course, is the regiment's famous Skull and Crossbones device with the motto 'Or Glory' below which can be seen in Image 5.

The year 1759 also saw the raising by Lord Aberdour of the 17th Edinburgh Light Dragoons, but as recruiting for this regiment did not go well it was disbanded in 1763. With this, Hale's 18th was then elevated to 17th position. For the period 1765 to 1769, when light dragoon regiments were listed in a separate sequence, the regiment was styled as the 3rd Light Dragoons.

The 17th crossed the Atlantic in 1775 upon the outbreak of hostilities in America and remained there until 1783. Artist Richard Simkin recalled this period via one of the full-page colour plates included with his *Our Armies* book of 1891. He gives the caption, 'The 17th Light Dragoons (now Lancers), on service in America 1775' and shows an officer wearing a scarlet coat with white collar, lapels and turnbacks. Silver lace adorns the front, collar and skirts, the shoulders having a small silver epaulette on each. A white waistcoat is just visible and white breeches fall into high black leather boots. The helmet is of black leather construction with a skull and crossbones plate and its long feather plume is red. A trumpeter rides by the officer's side who, by tradition, wears the regimental colours reversed—white coat with red facings, red waistcoat and breeches. His bicorn hat has a short white plume. Against a mountainous backdrop a troop gallops up a slope in response to the trumpeter's call. All in the picture except the trumpeter are mounted on brown horses. Both shabraques, the cloth that went under the saddle, are white with silver lace edging and carry the Royal Cypher and Crown together with a XVII LD regimental identification. The scarlet coats were replaced by blue in 1784.

2 – 17th Light Dragoons - Illustrated is a watercolour painting by Henry Heath (1801-58) belonging to the Anne SK Brown Military Collection which shows an officer of the 17th Light Dragoons. He wears a blue coat with two large gold epaulettes, two bars of gold lace each side of the white collar and gilt buttons down either side of the wide lapels. The wide trousers are of a blue-grey mixture decorated with wide gold lace, the girdle being made up of gold and crimson

5 - The Badge and its Wearer — 17th Lancers (Death or Glory Boys)

lines. Gold lace and cap lines decorate the shako which has a tall red and white feather plume.

In 1822 the 17th was deemed to be a lancer regiment, its title then appearing in the Army List as 17th Regiment of Light Dragoons (Lancers). Uniform authority WY Carman points out that the regiment was in India at the time and having returned home in 1823 the change from light dragoon dress to that of lancers, not to mention the necessary training in the use of the new weapon, would be gradual. But eventually in would come the lance-cap with its white cloth top, silver lace and flowing red and white feather plumes for officers. A less tall headdress was taken into use in 1828 which came with black plumes instead of red and white. The same year also seeing the blue-grey trousers replaced by an almost black type made of an Oxford mixture. *(Image courtesy of the Anne SK Brown Military Collection, Brown University Library)*

3 – 17th Light Dragoons (Lancers) - A lithograph plate after Michael Angelo Hayes (1820-1877) is illustrated which shows the 17th Light Dragoons (Lancers) in review order around 1840. Here, as the regiment parades, the regiment's blue coats and black plumes can be seen. Note how the horse furniture is also blue with gold edging and skull and crossbones insignia. The plate was part of a set published by William Spooner of 377 Strand, London, the printer being W Kohler who could be found at 22 Denmark Street, just off Charing Cross Road.

4 – Trooper - William IV in 1830 had a desire for all his regiments to be clothed in scarlet, his wish in the case of the 17th Light Dragoons being fulfilled over the following two years. But back came the blue in 1840. Illustrated is a PW Reynolds colour plate which shows a trooper in red coat and white trousers, the artist showing him in a short-tailed jacket with white collar, cuffs and skirt turnbacks. He wears a white leather pouch-belt, his headdress being decorated with gold cord, cap lines and black feather plume.

5 – The Badge And Its Wearer - In 1876, the regiment lost Light Dragoons from its title and in came the name of its colonel from 1842 to 1852, HRH George William Frederick Charles, 2nd Duke of Cambridge. The last illustration in this section is from Gale & Polden's 'The Badge and its Wearer' series of postcards and features an officer, his cap richly decorated with wide gold lace and cap lines and gilt fittings. The skull and crossbones badge is in silver on a gilt backing plate. Once used to clean out the touch-hole of a pistol or carbine, pickers were retained purely as ornaments by cavalry officers. Here we see them in silver hanging from chains on the pouch-belt.

18th (Queen Mary's Own) Hussars

Titles
1759 – 19th Light Dragoons
1763 – 18th Light Dragoons.
1807 – 18th Light Dragoons (Hussars). Disbanded in 1821
1858 – 18th Light Dragoons (Hussars)

1861 – 18th Hussars
1904 – 18th Princess of Wales's Hussars
1905 – 18th (Victoria Mary Princess of Wales's Own) Hussars
1910 – 18th (Queen Mary's Own Hussars)

Battle Honours
'Peninsula', 'Waterloo', 'Defence of Ladysmith', 'South Africa 1899-1902'

Recommended Further Reading
Colonel Harold Malet, *The Historical Memories of the XVIII Hussars (Princess of Wales's Own),* which was published in London by Simpkin & Co, Ltd, 1907. Contains seven colour plates of uniform.

Images

1 – Officer in Review Order, 1812 A 19th Light Dragoons was raised in Ireland by Charles, 1st Marquis of Drogheda in 1759. The corps, popularly known as the Drogheda Light Horse, was re-numbered as 18th Light Dragoons in 1763 and for the period 1766 to 1769 styled as the 4th Light Dragoons. During those years light dragoon regiments were numbered in a separate sequence. It was disbanded in Ireland as such in 1821, still with its original colonel, Lord Drogheda who died in December of the same year.

Little detail is known about the early uniform, historian WY Carman mentioning that an oil painting of officers exists which shows red coats with white half-lapels, silver lace and buttons. Helmets are black with gilt fittings and have a white ostrich plume on the left side. The GR cypher and White Horse of Hanover are displayed on the front of the headdress. At this period, notes WY Carman, officers wore a silver knot or strap on the right shoulder and a crimson sash over the left shoulder. Cavalry trumpeters usually wore hats; those of the 18th Hussars have been, however, noted as wearing helmets. White also formed the colour of the lining, breeches and waistcoat. A special distinction regarding the latter, records Mr Carman, was its scarlet edging. Blue jackets with white facings replaced the red in 1784 and gradually hussar details in the uniform began to appear, such as rows of silver or white braid on the chest and a pelisse. With the re-styling as hussars in 1807 came a brown fur busby which had a light blue bag and tall scarlet and white plume.

The Anne SK Brown Military Collection have an original watercolour by Charles Lydall depicting an officer in review order in 1812. A gold and crimson cord encircles the brown busby, the same pattern hanging down from the sash and sword hilt. The officer's blue jacket is adorned with silver or white lace across the chest, his white collar and cuffs trimmed with the same. Hanging over the left shoulder, the blue pelisse is trimmed with a thick grey fur all around.

2 – Private, 18th Light Dragoons (Hussars) In this detailed print published in May 1912 after Charles Hamilton Smith, we see a private of the regiment wearing a blue pelisse slung over the left shoulder which has thick white fur around the collar, down the front and around the lower edge. He wears white breeches and a brown fur busby with white-over-red plume, brass chin scales and a light blue bag. Note how the latter seems to be affixed to the centre

of the headdress then droops down to several inches below the rim. Shabraques, with this white pointed border design, were often referred to as 'Vandycked'.

3 – Captain Flood Sharpe The Anne SK Brown Military Collection is also in possession of another fine work, this time by William Heath (1795-1840), which shows what they believe to be a portrait of a Captain William Edward or Robert Anthony Flood Sharpe. He is shown standing holding a brown fur busby in the right hand which has a tall white plume with a red base, gold lines and a blue busby bag. The jacket and white-fur-edged pelisse are of a much darker blue than in the Lydall image above, both garments being richly decorated with silver braid and cord. The wide overalls are now light grey. Both the collar and cuffs are white with silver decoration. The officer has a gold and crimson barrelled girdle and a blue-faced sabretache with wide silver lace on all four sides. There seems to be no decoration other than a crown above a 'GR' cypher within a wreath. The artist dates the picture as c1818.

4 – Officer, 1869 When the 18th Hussars were re-formed in Leeds in 1858, the uniform adopted was dark blue with a distinctive Lincoln green colour used

for the busby bags and plumes. For details, we can turn to Dress Regulations which gives: '*Jacket* – tunic, entirely of blue cloth; single-breasted; the collar two inches high, rounded in front. On each side of the breast, six loops of gold chain lace, with caps and drops, fastening with six gold worked olivets: the top loop eight inches long, the bottom one four inches. The jacket edged all round (except the collar) with gold chain lace.' Unseen in the painting is the back of the jacket which has: 'On the back seams a double chain of the same lace, edged with braid forming three eyes at top, passing under a netted cap at the waist, and terminating in a knot at bottom of skirt.'

In this 1869-dated print after PW Reynolds, the artist has formed his image true to the preceding description from Dress Regulations. The gold lace mentioned also forming the Austrian knot on the sleeve. The pouch-belt is also of gold lace, on a scarlet ground, and has silver ornaments. The same scarlet colour forms the face of the sabretache, which has wide gold lace on three sides and displays a crowned 'VR' cypher.

Referring to the busby cap, Dress Regulations mention that its black sable fur should fall half an inch all round below the body of the framework. The oval cockade is of gold gimp, the green busby bag having lines of gold braid which form a junction at the bottom. Here a gold gimp one-inch button is placed.

In 1878, and to reflect the connection with the former 18th, permission was given to replace the green busby bags with one of blue. The plumes at the same time changed to white over a red base.

19th (Queen Alexandra's Own Royal) Hussars

Titles
1759 – 19th Light Dragoons
1763 – 18th Dragoons. Disbanded as Hussars in 1821
1779 – 19th Light Dragoons. Disbanded in 1783
1781 – 23rd Light Dragoons
1786 – 19th Light Dragoons
1817 – 19th Lancers. Disbanded in 1821
1858 – 1st Bengal European Cavalry
1861 – 19th Light Dragoons. Renamed as 19th Hussars in the same year
1885 – 19th (Princess of Wales's Own) Hussars
1902 – 19th (Alexandra Princess of Wales's Own) Hussars
1908 – 19th (Queen Alexandra's Own Royal) Hussars

Battle Honours
'Assaye', 'Mysore', 'Seringapatam', 'Niagara', 'Tel-el-Kabir', 'Egypt 1882-1884', 'Abu Klea', 'Nile 1884-85', 'Defence of Ladysmith', 'South Africa 1899-1902'

Recommended Further Reading
Colonel John Biddulph, *The Nineteenth and their Times; Being an Account of the Four Cavalry Regiments in the British Army that have borne the number Nineteen and of the Campaigns in which they Served* which was published in London by John Murray in 1899. Contains three colour plates of uniform and one of guidon.

Images
1 – 19th Light Dragoons, 1792 Very little is known, points out uniform authority WY Carman, of the 1779-83 period 19th Light Dragoons, save that red coats with green lapels were worn, the officers having silver lace. For the 23rd Light Dragoons raised in 1781, the same author notes that the authorised dress was red with dark green facings and white linings. The officers' lace and buttons were silver, the other ranks having white metal. The waistcoats and breeches were white.

Blue coats were ordered for light dragoon regiments in 1784 and here, in this original watercolour by Charles

James Lyall (1845-1920) dated 1792 we see a member of the 19th Light Dragoons wearing a short light blue jacket with yellow collar and cuffs edged with white lace. Five double rows of white cord running across the chest are visible, a sixth being out of sight under a crimson waist sash knotted on the right side. The black leather helmet has a red (or orange possibly) main flowing down from a gilt crest and a leopard skin turban. *(Image courtesy of the Anne SK Brown Military Collection, Brown University Library)*

2 - 19th Lancers - When raised in 1781, the regiment first appeared under the title of 23rd Light Dragoons. It was re-numbered as 19th in 1786 and served in India throughout the twenty-five years following is formation. While there it fought at Assaye in September 1803, the battle honour for this engagement not being authorised until four years later. A badge of an elephant was granted at the same time. When the 69th Regiment found itself down to its last cartridge during a sepoy mutiny at Vellore in 1806, it was a detachment of the 19th that came to the rescue of the few men that remained. From Ireland in 1813 the regiment was sent to America where it gained the battle honour 'Niagara' in 1815. Added to this in 1818, and somewhat late it might be said, was 'Seringapatam' recalling the capture of that place on 3 May 1799. The 19th Light Dragoons became 19th Lancers in 1816, only to be disbanded five years later in August 1821.

The Anne SK Brown Military Collection at Brown University Library are in possession of a watercolour by Henry Warren (1794-1879) measuring 38.2 x 24.4 cm which features a member of the regiment. His jacket is blue with yellow collar, lapels and cuffs. He wears grey overalls with a narrow yellow stripe and a blue and yellow girdle. The cap is yellow with a gilt plate and white and red plume, the lines running down from the rear and around to the front of the jacket. Un-detailed in the image are the domed buttons which show crossed lances with a crown above

and the numeral XIX below. Also not shown in the painting is the sabretache which had a crown over the 'GR' cypher, the battle honour 'Assaye' and the silver elephant badge which was authorized with that award, 'Niagara' and crossed lances. A lance cap exists which has a front plate bearing the royal arms. The trousers were changed to blue before disbandment in September 1821. *(Image courtesy of the Anne SK Brown Military Collection, Brown University Library)*

3 – 19th Hussars, c1890 This image is taken from Supplement No 29 produced for the *Army and Navy Gazette* from artwork supplied by Richard Simkin and published on 3 May 1890. Here we see a tunic of blue cloth, edged all round with gold chain gimp. The collar is edged along the top with ¾-inch lace and each side of the breast has six loops of gold chain gimp. The same material has been used to form the Austrian knots on each sleeve and the shoulder cords, which are lined with blue cloth. The busby is of black sable fur with a gold oval cockade, and a fifteen-inch ostrich feather plume. Just visible in the painting is the regiment's distinctive white busby bag.

It was not until 1874 that the 'Assaye' battle honour, and along with it the badge of an elephant, earnt by the regiment's predecessor on 23 September 1803, was permitted to be displayed. Here we see it placed below the crown and 'VR' cypher on the sabretache, which has a scarlet face and gold lace with a white silk central stripe around three sides.

4 – The Badges and Their Wearer A complete change of uniform in this postcard after Harry Payne. From one of the 'Oilette' series published by Raphael Tuck & Sons Ltd, the card shows a member of the 19th Hussars placing a clip of five .303 rounds into a bandolier. He wears khaki service dress, his cap having the white metal badge seen in the top left-hand corner of the postcard.

The badge takes the form of a letter 'A' surmounted by a crown, the cypher of Queen Alexandra, interwoven with a cross inscribed with the date 1885 and overlapped by the name Alexandra. The cross is the Dannebrog Cross, a Danish Order of chivalry, the date that of the year in which the regiment had taken on the name of Princess Alexandria. Her father, the king of Denmark, her husband, the Prince of Wales, she would become Queen Alexandria upon the death of Queen Victoria in 1901. The actual change to the badge shown, which seems to have been painted with the wrong date by ten years, was not until 1909. Prior to that, the elephant appears on the headdress.

20TH HUSSARS

TITLES
1759 – 20th Inniskilling Light Dragoons. Disbanded in 1763
1779 – 20th Light Dragoons. Disbanded in 1783
1791 – 20th Jamaica Light Dragoons
1802 – 20th Light Dragoons. Disbanded in 1818
1858 – 2nd Bengal European Light Cavalry
1861 – 20th Light Dragoons
1862 – 20th Hussars

BATTLE HONOURS
'Vimiera', 'Peninsula', 'Suakin 1885', 'South Africa 1901-02'

RECOMMENDED FURTHER READING
Lieutenant-Colonel LB Oatts, *Emperor's Chambermaids, The Story of the 14th/20th Kings Hussars.* London, Ward Lock, 1973.

IMAGES
1 – Lieutenant George William Adolphus FitzGeorge The first of the cavalry regiments to hold the number 20th was formed in Ireland in 1759 from part of the 6th Inniskilling Dragoons. That regiment was wearing yellow facings at the time and it is thought that this colour continued with the new 20th Inniskilling Light Dragoons. Henry Manners Chichester and George Burges-Short in their 1900 book, *The Records and Badges of Every Regiment and Corps of the British Army,* note that scarlet jackets were worn, the facings changing at some time from yellow to black before disbandment in 1763.

For the second regiment, that raised in 1779 and disbanded in 1783, a contemporary Army List gives yellow facings, the coats, it is thought, being scarlet and with silver lace. Next, in 1791, came the 20th Jamaica Light Dragoons which lost the 'Jamaica' part of its title in 1802. Disbandment came in 1818. It had been raised in Ireland for service in Jamaica and wore dark blue jackets with yellow (later orange) facings. The badge of a crocodile, from the country's coat of arms, was worn as a badge.

Image 1 features George William Adolphus FitzGeorge, the eldest son of the 2nd Duke of Cambridge who we see in the uniform of a lieutenant, 20th Hussars. He had purchased a commission in 1861 and went on to serve on the personal staff of General Sir Garnet Wolseley during the Egyptian Campaign of 1882. He retired from the army with the rank of colonel in 1895 and died twelve years later in Lucerne. Dated 1870, the image is by HJ Walker and shows an all dark blue, hussar style, uniform decorated with gold lace. The colour crimson was a regimental distinction and we see it here on the pouch-belt sword and sabretache straps. Crimson too for the sabretache face, which is embellished with gold lace, the royal cypher below a crown, '20H' within a circle and the single battle honour 'Peninsula' on a scroll. The black sable busby has a tall crimson feather plume, gold cords and fittings and a crimson bag which has three gold lace lines running to the bottom, at the junction of which is placed a gold button. The officer's rank is indicated by the gold Austrian knot sleeve decoration and the single star on each collar. *(Image courtesy of the Anne SK Brown Military Collection, Brown University Library)*

2 – Mounted Officer, c1890 From Richard Simkin's 'Military Types' series produced as supplements to the *Army* *and Navy Gazette,* we have No 30 in the set which features a mounted officer of the 20th Hussars. Published on 7 June 1890, the image shows the officer in much the same dress as Image 1 above. Here again is the all blue uniform, gold lace and crimson busy bag and plume, Simkin this time giving a better interpretation of the gold cap lines and silver ornaments affixed to the pouch-belt—the pickers were once used to clean the touch-hole of a pistol or carbine but now purely for decoration. The gold-laced belt has a crimson silk half-inch stripe running through its centre. Mounted officers at this time were seated on leopard skins edged with crimson. Crimson too for the horse's throat plume.

3 – Two Mounted Officers, c1892 So as to perpetuate the facings of the old 20th Light Dragoons, in 1892 the regiment's crimson headdress plumes were exchanged for the yellow as seen in this original watercolour by Richard Simkin. According to the 1900 edition of *Dress Regulations for Officers of the Army*, the plumes were: 'Ostrich feather, 15 inches high from the top of the busby to the top of the plume; encircled by a ring. Vulture feather bottom in a corded gilt ball socket with four upright leaves.' The horse's throat plumes were also affected by the same change. Just visible in the background of the picture are several other ranks, noticeable by their much shorter busby plumes and the carbines attached by slings to their saddles. *(Image courtesy of the Anne SK Brown Military Collection, Brown University Library)*

4 – Kettledrummer WJ Gordon's c1914 book, *Bands of the British Army*, includes an illustrated representation (artwork by Frederick Stansell) of every cavalry drum horse in the British Army. The drum horse seen here is a grey, its kettledrummer a lance-corporal. The crimson drum banner, with its 'VR' cypher, is displayed above the battle honour 'Peninsular' which, together with 'Vimiera' seen of the left, were distinctions awarded to the 20th Light Dragoons of the 1791-18 period. To the right, and unseen in the image, is the honour 'Suakin 1885'. Here too is the yellow throat ornament as part of the horse furniture, and the other ranks' stiff yellow hair busby plume, which is shorter than that worn by the officers.

Historian RG Harris produced a number of articles entitled, 'Mounted Bands, Their Drum Horses and Banners', for the Military Historical Society during the 1960s and it is from that series that we hear how new drum banners had certainly been obtained by the regiment after the award of the 'Suakin' battle honour in 1886. 'In 1889', records RG Harris, the 20th Hussars obtained a splendid four-year-old horse from the Remount Depot in Ireland.' He goes on to say that after training as a drum horse, the animal was seen on parade in London in 1890.

'In October, 1895' (RG Harris again), 'the regiment handed over its drum-horse to the 3rd Dragoon Guards before sailing for India, where it remained until the South African War broke out.' It would seem that the horse described by Harris was that on which Frederick Stansell had based his painting.

21st (Empress of India's) Lancers

Titles
1759 – 21st Light Dragoons or Royal Windsor Foresters. Disbanded in 1763
1779 – 21st Light Dragoons. Disbanded in 1783
1794 – 21st Light Dragoons. Disbanded in 1820
1858 – 3rd Bengal European Light Cavalry
1861 – 21st Light Dragoons, later the same year changing to 21st Hussars
1897 – 21st Lancers
1898 – 21st (Empress of India's) Lancers

Battle Honour
'Khartoum'

Recommended Further Reding
Major RLC Tamplin, *Death or Glory, A Short History of the 17th/21st Lancers* which was published in Nairobi by the regiment in 1959. A 100-page record with two colour plates of uniform.

Images

1 – 21st Light Dragoons, Royal Windsor Foresters There had been three regiments with the title 21st Light Dragoons prior to the transfer to the British Crown of the 3rd Bengal European Light Cavalry from the East India Company's forces in 1861. Also known as the Royal Windsor Foresters, the first was raised by John Manners, Marquis of Granby in April 1759. Henry Manners Chichester and George Burges-Short note in their book *The Records and Badges of Every Regiment and Corps in the British Army*, that writers of the period had described the regiment as one of the finest corps in the country's service. It was disbanded in 1763.

The next regiment to bear the title of 21st Light Dragoons was that raised during American War from members of the 3rd, 4th and 7th Dragoons. Disbandment came in 1783 having seen no overseas service. The corps raised in 1794 did, however, and a troop was part of the force sent to guard Napoleon after the French emperor had been sent to St Helena. The regiment, which was also known as the 21st Yorkshire Light Dragoons due to its formation in the north of England, returned home from India and afterwards disbanded at Chatham in 1820. The St Helena troop, however, remained until Napoleon's death in 1821.

In this original watercolour by Reginald Augustus Wymer (1849-1835) painted in 1899, we see a member of the regiment in a long scarlet coat with a dark blue turned down collar, lapels running down to the waist, and cuffs. The button holes are edged with silver lace and there is a silver epaulette being worn on the right shoulder. The white waistcoat has round silver buttons. The headdress device is not clear in Wymer's artwork, but a preserved helmet belonging to the regiment has been noted which has a metal plate bearing a crown over 'GR' and the letters 'R' and 'F'. *(Image courtesy of the ASK Brown Military Collection, Brown University Library)*

2 – 21st Hussars With the transfer of the 3rd Bengal European Light Cavalry to the British Establishment in 1861,

the title assumed was 21st Light Dragoons, but in August of that year the regiment was named as Hussars. With this came a uniform consisting of a fur busby which had a French-grey bag on the right side. The colour chosen as a commemoration of the uniform previously worn by the 3rd Bengal. The tall plume was white. The illustration shows an officer, the plumes of which were feathers, those for the other ranks being hair. Gold lace decorates the dark blue jacket, breeches and sabretache. The latter, however, had a scarlet face until 1876. The horse furniture includes a leopard skin saddlecloth and white throat-plume. The illustration is an original watercolour by Richard Simkin. *(Image courtesy of the Anne SK Brown Military Collection, Brown University Library)*

3 – The Battle of Omdurman The heroic action of the 21st Lancers at Omdurman on 2 September 1898 has now gone down on record as the last operational cavalry charge by British troops. Also of note is that among the 400 that took part was none other than one Lieutenant Winston Churchill, later politician and Prime Minister of Great Britain. British commander, Sir Herbert Kitchener was anxious to take control of Omdurman ahead of the city being occupied by the enemy's forces. Sent ahead to clear the path was the 21st Lancers who had been told that resistance would only take the form of a few hundred dervishes. They would meet, however, a force 2,500 strong. In the resulting action, seen here depicted in a print after Stanley Berkeley, a fierce fight took place in which the enemy were successfully

KETTLE-DRUMMER
21ST (EMPRESS OF INDIA'S) LANCERS, C1912

driven back by the lancers. Subsequently, three of the regiment received Victoria Crosses: Captain Paul Aloysius Kenna, Lieutenant Raymond de Montgomery and Private Thomas Byrne, and the regiment, the battle honour 'Khartoum'. Note the French-grey helmet Puggarees. Published by Henry Graves & Co, the image measures 96.8 x 68 cm.

4 – 21st Lancers, Kettle-Drummer c1912 The 21st Hussars were serving in India in 1897 when news was received of its conversion to Lancers. Soon the Army List would record the regiment as wearing blue uniforms with scarlet facings and white plumes in the new lance caps. However, notes uniform authority WC Carman, it was quite possible that, although pictures were produced, a full dress uniform of this type was never worn. It was while serving in Egypt in 1898 that a special order was received informing the regiment of its change in title to 21st (Empress of India's) Lancers. Soon after, the French-grey long associated with the regiment as hussars, was restored and the cypher 'VRI' authorised as a badge.

In Richard Simkin's study of a kettle-drummer around 1912, French-grey is much in evidence at the top of the lance cap, for the collar and plastron. Note how the headdress white plume has been crimped, a tradition in the band since the time of Edward VII. Simkin includes great detail with his depiction of both the drum-banner and saddle cloth. The regimental badge with crossed lances on each, the drum-banner also having a Union wreath of roses, thistles and shamrocks, and the regiment's 'Khartoum' battle honour. The horse furniture also includes a white throat-plume and a black lambskin edged with French-grey. Interestingly, the unseen banner on the drummer's right side was different in respect that it displayed a royal coat of arms, complete with royal crest and lion and unicorn supporters, together with a scroll bearing the title of the regiment.

5 – The Despatch Orderlies Less well known than military artist Harry Payne, was his brother Arthur. Also an accomplished painter who often worked with Harry on pictures, Arthur specialised in architectural detail and it is from his brushes that the building in the background of this Raphael Tuck & Sons postcard originated—Wren's Marlborough House, completed in 1711 and from time to time used as a Royal residence in London.

BIBLIOGRAPHY

All the books referred to in the 'Recommended Further Reading' sections of this Guide have been consulted. Also the following:

Army List. Several editions from 1740 to 1914

Army Museums Ogilby Trust. *Index to British Military Costume Prints 1500-1914.* London 1972

Carman, WY. *Richard Simkin's Uniforms of the British Army – The Cavalry Regiments.* Webb & Brewer, Exeter, 1982

Carman, WT. *The Ackermann Military Prints - Uniforms of the British & Indian Armies 1840-1858.* Schiffer Military History, Atglen, USA, 2003

Harrington, Peter. *British Army Uniforms in Colour.* Schiffer Military History, Atglen, USA, 2001

Haswell Miller, AE and NP Dawnay. *Military Drawings and Paintings in the Collection of Her Majesty the Queen.* Phaidon Press, London, 1966 and 1969

Haythornthwaite, Philip J. *Wellington's Army The Uniforms of the British Soldier, 1812-1815.* Greenhill Books, London, 2002

Lawson, Cecil CP. *A History of The Uniforms of the British Army,* Volumes 1 to 5. Several publishers between 1940 and 1967

Parkyn, Major HG. *(Military) Shoulder-Belt Plates and Buttons.* Gale & Polden, Aldershot, 1956

Journal of the Society for Army Historical Research. Several issues from 1921 to 1980

RAY WESTLAKE'S GUIDES TO THE BRITISH ARMY

A Series of British Army Reference Books

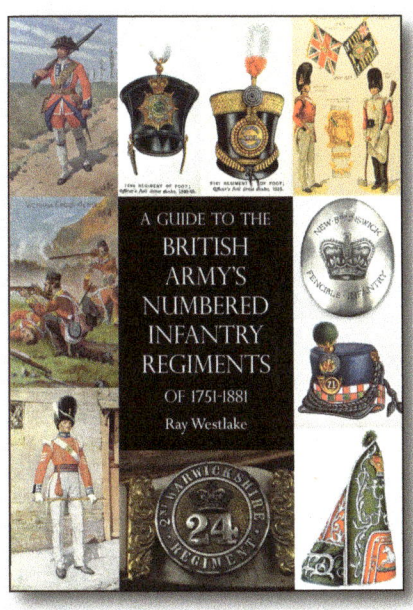

New "Westlake" classics!

Ray's series of British Army 'Guides' fill an important gap by placing succinct information on the subject matter in an accessible manner.

FULL COLOUR ILLUSTRATIONS THROUGHOUT EACH VOLUME

www.naval-military-press.com

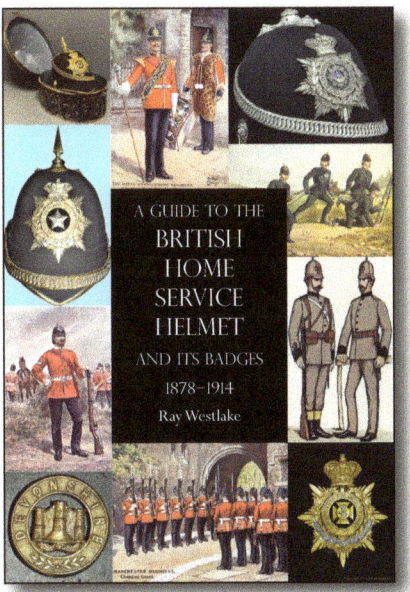

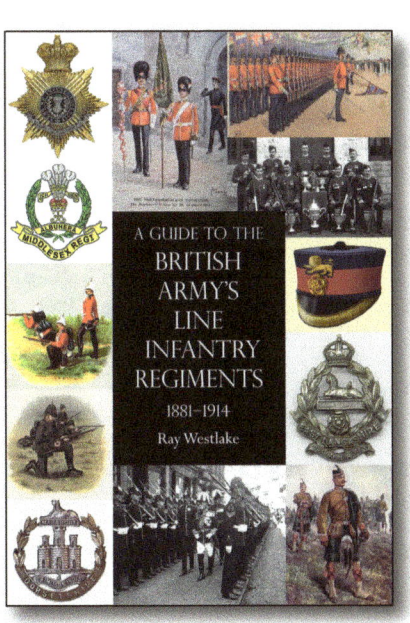

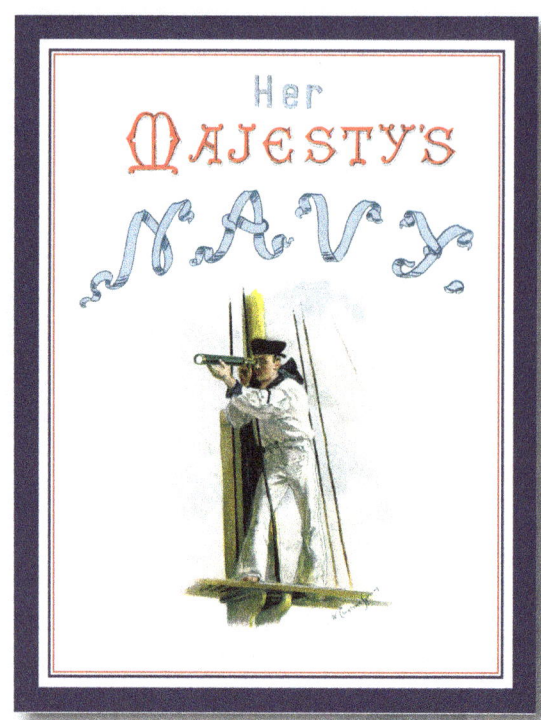

HER MAJESTY'S NAVY 1890

Including Its Deeds And Battles

The companion volumes to
HER MAJESTY'S ARMY 1888 –
HER MAJESTY'S NAVY 1890
with text by Charles Rathbone Low, overflowing with excellent plates of exceptional quality, both of ship portraits and sailors' costumes.

A fascinating study of the British Navy, that is copiously illustrated throughout, and complete in three volumes. Of particular note are the ship portraits by W. Fred Mitchell that include Victory, Captain, Thrush, Speedwell, Blenheim, Royal Sovereign and others (with emphasis on the Ironclad period). Many of the original artworks reproduced in this work are held by the National Maritime Museum Collection in Greenwich.

Softback edition in 3 volumes
1210 pages in total
+ 41 colour uniform plates
printed on 70lbs paper
Product code: 28738

Hardback edition in 3 volumes
1210 pages in total
+ 41 colour uniform plates
printed on 70lbs paper
Product code: 28738HB

HER MAJESTY'S ARMY 1888

A descriptive account of the various regiments now comprising the Queen's Forces & Indian and Colonial Forces

This is a much sought-after three-volume set – the first two are devoted entirely to the British Army, with the third to India and the Colonies, all from their first establishment to the 'present time', c.1888. The author's main aim was to describe the organisation and condition of each unit as it was in the 1880s.

Consisting of written sketches of the various regiments, they contain much useful information on their battles, campaigns and prior fighting achievements, complemented **with 41 excellent, full-page chromolithographic uniform plates**.

The plates in the first two volumes are by G.D. Giles who saw service with the British Army in India, Afghanistan and Egypt; those of the Indian and Colonial forces volume are by H. Bunnett. This work was originally published c.1888 by J.S. Virtue & Co Ltd, a London publishing business, the main feature of which was the production of illustrated works.

**Softback edition in 3 volumes
1210 pages in total
+ 41 colour uniform plates
printed on 70lbs paper
Product code: 28703**

**Hardback edition in 3 volumes
1210 pages in total
+ 41 colour uniform plates
printed on 70lbs paper
Product code: 28703HB**

HEAD-DRESS BADGES OF THE BRITISH ARMY VOL 1. 1800-1918
ISBN 9781843425120

Illustrated record of badges worn on every type of head-dress from the mitre cap to the Shako to the Field Service cap, with detailed comments. Changes in regimental title and dates of amalgamations given. Starts in the year 1800.

HEAD-DRESS BADGES OF THE BRITISH ARMY VOL 2. 1919-1979
ISBN 9781843425137

From end of the Great War to 1979. Includes OTC badges and all special units raised in WWII as well as those of the Gurkha regiments.

Following the death of Hugh King and the disposal of his collection by auction. The Naval and Military Press reissued both volumes of his and L Kipling's work. First published in the seventies they still remain the bible for all serious badge collectors. Intended as the standard reference, these two volumes are a record of badges worn on every type of head-dress from the mitre cap to the Shako to the Field Service cap, with complete with detailed comments and identifier photographs. Changes in regimental title and dates of amalgamations given.

It should be noted that dealers and auctioneers refer to Kipling and King numbers for identification purposes.

www.ingramcontent.com/pod-product-compliance
Lightning Source LLC
Chambersburg PA
CBHW040316240426
43663CB00026B/2979